Time to Act!
The Enemy Snuck in
While We Were Sleeping

Dr. Douglas E. Carr

Copyright Reformation Day 2022
Revised for better clarity February 2023
© Dr. Douglas E. Carr

Published by Doug Carr Freedom Ministry

Printed by KDP

ISBN: 978-1-7366952-5-8

Bible Translations Used

Dedication

I dedicate this book to all those, past and present, who have made the choice to take up their cross daily and follow the Lord Jesus all the way into God's will, regardless of how others respond.

I dedicate it to those who risk their lives to keep their communities and countries safe. Police who travel their cities, not knowing what might await them. People in the armed services who risk their lives to secure our freedom and safety.

I dedicate it to mothers and fathers who pay the price to assure children are taught value and responsibility.

I dedicate this book to pastors and preachers who teach what the Bible says and refuse to tickle the ears of people hoping to build large crowds of people who will also lack conviction.

I dedicate it to teachers and professors who teach truth, history, and values in an atmosphere where WOKE and unbiblical philosophies are not only accepted but expected by liberal politicians and school boards.

Most of all, I dedicate this book to my wife, partner, co-pastor, and best friend, Pamela Jo Carr. She is a woman who loves God and people so much she sacrifices much to bless others. I admire her strong conviction God is able to move mountains when we speak to them in faith.

I wrote this dedication on my birthday, Reformation Day, October 31. Therefore, I dedicate this book to every reformer who has followed the call and commitment of Martin Luther who posted his ninety-five theses of the Wittenberg's Castle Church on October 31, 1517. May today's reformers again take their stand and change the course of society.

Acknowledgments

Suzanne LeBlanc continues to faithfully edit my books. Even though she provides daily care for her aging mother who suffers from time-consuming needs, Suzanne manages to create power points and provide editing services for my books.

The leaders who are part of our Michiana Breakthrough Apostolic Ministry Network are greater support to Pam and I than they will ever realize this side of heaven. Their involvement in monthly regional meetings is a great encouragement. Heaven comes down and kisses earth when this group prays! Together, we seek strategies to release revival in our Michigan/Indiana region.

His House Foursquare Church is comprised of the most loving and dedicated congregation we have ever pastored. They believe in God for big things and are not afraid of deliverance, letting Holy Spirit move, prophetic words, and divine healing. Pam and I are blessed to pastor such a loving, giving, and forgiving congregation.

I also acknowledge the people who come to us for Deliverance and Deep Healing ministry. We learn from everyone we meet. Many are survivors who have pressed through trials and trauma that might have destroyed others.

Finally, I acknowledge those who have completed or are going through our Deliverance Ministers Equipping and Certification program. They truly are becoming a well-equipped army fit for the Master's use to set all the captives free who will soon become part of the church through the Great Awakening which will soon be released in our country and world.

The Kingdom of God is advancing forcibly through people whose callings stretch them beyond all they can think, hope, and imagine according to the resurrection power of Jesus Christ who dwells within them.

Contents

Dedication		v
Acknowledgments		vii
Foreword		x
Author's Preface		xx
1	Why It Matters Now	24
2	Suit up for Battle! The Enemy is at the Door	28
3	War Over the Shedding of Innocent Blood	43
4	The War for Biblical Marriage	65
5	WOKE or Wake Up?	84
6	Amendment to Title IX	92
7	Power to Complete Our Mission	99
8	What I hear God saying for 5783 and beyond	107
9	The Greatest of These . . . in a WOKE Culture	116
10	It is Time to Identify the Real Enemy	132
	Final Thoughts	150
	About the Author	152
	Resources	156

Foreword by Suzanne LeBlanc

The Power of Prayer and Proclamation

Prayer activates the impossible in our lives, for what we deem impossible to do is possible with God. When we partner with God in prayer, we are no longer bound by the limitations of this earth. Everything is possible, and life becomes exciting because our ways become His ways, our thoughts become His thoughts. In prayer, we can hear what is on the heart of the Father and declare it so into the earthly realm, "You will also declare a thing, and it will be established for you; so light will shine on your ways" (Job 22:28).

Let me emphasize that God will not do anything without a praying person to partner with here on earth. "So I sought for a man among them who would make a wall, and stand in the gap before Me on behalf of the land, that I should not destroy it; but I found no one" (Ezekiel 22:30). God desires that we partner with Him to bring heaven to earth, to bring restoration and healing to people and the land. In 2 Chronicles 7:14, God declares, "If My people who are called by My name will humble themselves, and pray and seek My face, and turn from their wicked ways, then I will hear from heaven, and will forgive their sin and heal their land."

The greatest miracle is salvation. When we repent in prayer, renounce our wicked ways, and ask Jesus to rule and reign our lives and we offer our lives as a living sacrifice. Then and only then is the work of Calvary activated in us and we are covered by the blood of Jesus, so we can be restored unto the Father. At that moment we are translated into the Kingdom of God and are given eternal life. God is longsuffering toward us, not willing that any should perish but that all should come to repentance (2 Peter 3:9). God is able to save all who call upon the name of Jesus. Sin—whether it be a lie or murder—is sin, and it separates us from God. At the moment of salvation, Jesus indwells in our spirit, and via Holy Spirit we are empowered to do God's will and all that He has called us to do. What a precious gift! We become children of God with an eternal inheritance.

God is so good, gracious, and merciful towards us, and the more you get to know God, the more you're undone by His mercy. In September of 2000, my sister, Cherie, went missing. She was 29 years old, an adult, so the police were hesitant to search for her within the first 24 hours of her disappearance. My parents were frantic, and my mom called me to pray, so I quieted myself to pray, and that's when the Lord commanded, "Emergency Prayer Chain NOW!" Those words cut straight into my spirit like lightening. It was 10:45 PM, so I called Lilly Stewart who manned the Kalamazoo

First Assembly of God Prayer Chain 24 x 7. We prayed. Several days later, my sister's body was found in an abandoned home; she had been brutally murdered. My family was devastated. Did God hear our prayers?

It wasn't until recently that I learned how God answered those prayers. In March of 2001, while in the courtroom listening to the testimony from the kids who witnessed my sister's final moments, I had a vision. While Cherie was being beaten, I saw her spirit leave her body to go and talk with Jesus, but I could not hear what they were talking about. Then I saw Cherie leave with Jesus. Now, I always wondered what they had talked about, but I knew that I knew it had something to do with her salvation, but I never quite understood that because Cherie had always talked about Jesus from time to time. Cherie was living a back-slidden life like the rest of us. We did not know any different. Only years later, I would understand how we are to live for Jesus, pick up our cross daily, and let Jesus rule and reign in our lives; we are to live transformed lives by the grace of God, for sin no longer has a hold on us. We are to be daily transformed into the image of Jesus Christ—the former life now gone. "But we all, with unveiled face, beholding as in a mirror the glory of the Lord, are being transformed into the same image from glory to glory, just as by the Spirit of the Lord" (2 Corinthians 3:18).

So, what happened in Cherie's final moments? I believe Jesus showed up before she died. I know God wants no one to perish. I asked the Lord for reassurance, and I heard, "your prayers are not in vain." We find confirmation in 1 Corinthians 15:58, "Therefore, my beloved brothers and sisters, be steadfast, immovable, always excelling in the work of the Lord [always doing your best and doing more than is needed], being continually aware that your labor [even to the point of exhaustion] in the Lord is not futile nor wasted [it is never without purpose]." Prayers are not empty, worthless, or ineffective, but powerful, yielding the miraculous, and the greatest miracle of all is salvation.

In February of 2021, when I heard of the murder of my neighbors, Laura and Gary Johnson, and that their son, Nicholas, now 27 years old, was held in the county jail as suspect, I was overcome by the heart of God with great compassion for their son Nick whom I have known since the age of 7. I could still see him as a small boy, playing with his toys. No matter how great the sin, God's heart is that none should perish, for we have all fallen short of the glory of God. In that instant, I knew God needed an intercessor for Nick, and I told the Lord that I would pray for his salvation for God to transform his life and use him whether in prison or not. Truly, God requires us to partner with Him in prayer. The burden to pray for someone may overtake us while we are awake, or even while we are asleep, dreaming. I recall many times praying in a dream for people in different countries that I have never met this side of heaven. Only in eternity, will I know the full impact of those prayers, for we do not pray in vain. Amen!

"And these signs will follow those who believe: In My name they will cast out demons; they will speak with new tongues;" (Mark 16:17). We can pray in our natural, earthly language, or in a spiritual, God-given heavenly language as described in the book of Acts. "And they were all filled with the Holy Spirit and began to speak with other tongues, as the Spirit gave them utterance" (Acts 2:4). When we pray in the spirit in tongues, we do not speak to men, "but to God, for no one understands him; however, in the spirit he speaks mysteries," 1 Corinthians 14:2. Yes, we do pray mysteries. Even the kingdom of darkness does not understand what we pray when we pray in tongues—and this was never so evident to me until one morning in July 2019 while in prayer. I was praying for God's will to be done in the White House for our nation in my earthly tongue (English) when a cluster of brown-gray rats appeared to me in the Spirit, listening to every word I was praying. Suddenly, I was compelled to pray in tongues, and when I did. The rats could no longer understand what I was praying, so they fled. That morning I touched based with another intercessor, and I asked if she was seeing rats while praying; she said no, but other intercessors were seeing rats when praying for the White House. On July 29, 2019, the Washington Post wrote an article, entitled "The Vermin in the White House," about the literal rat-infestation in the White House, for what happens in the natural world will be addressed in the spiritual world. As the rats are removed in the natural, so will it be accomplished in the spiritual realm via the power of prayer. Praise God! For it is time for the rat-driven, demonic agenda be abolished in the White House, and that God's will be accomplished in the White House for this nation.

What we pray is just as vital as to how we pray, "for death and life are in the power of the tongue, and those who love it will eat its fruit" (Proverbs 18:21). We need to align our prayers with the Word of God, so that God's will for what we are praying for can be accomplished God's way and not our way. Many prayers are not answered because the motive of the heart does not align with the will of God. How do we know what God's will is? We know it by reading the Word of God in order to know the heart of the God of the Word. While my daughter, Sarah, was expecting her forth baby, we were praying for a baby girl since she already has three boys. She and her husband Aaron's plan was to have one more child, that it be a girl, and they would be done having children.

God, however, answered her prayer and showed her in a dream she would have a baby girl as the fifth child, not the fourth, for God had a plan and a purpose for Seth Jeremiah to be born. "People can plan what they want to do, but it is the Lord who guides their steps" (Proverbs 16:9, ERV). Amen!

In 2007, I was tormented with dreams of my parents being killed by drug dealers night after night. Why? Because it was a possibility as a result of my brother's drug addiction that was grossly out of hand. As I interceded for God to do something, the nightmares grew more intense and real. In fact, I was quite shaken by them. However, after several months of these tormenting dreams, I finally got angry at the devil and declared, "No, they will not die like that!" I decreed that they will be protected by God and His angel armies. I had to formally reject the picture coming from the pit of hell by speaking out loud, proclaiming what God had for them night after night. The battle was brutal, and it went on for months; each time I woke up and declared the opposite of what Satan was projecting, and little by little the tormenting dreams subsided. I prayed for a plan, and God made a way when there was no way for my parents to move into my home, now relocated far from danger. Prayer can stop hell's agenda for your family and establish the godly vision through the power of your words.

Make prayer time a routine appointment with God. Peter and John kept their prayer appointment with God at the nineth hour in the temple (Acts 3:1). Daniel prayed three times daily. "And in his upper room, with his windows open toward Jerusalem, he knelt down on his knees three times that day, and prayed and gave thanks before his God, as was his custom since early days" (Daniel 6:10). David, the psalmist, prayed seven times daily, praising God. "Seven times a day I praise You, Because of Your righteous judgments" (Psalm 119:164). People who greatly impact the Kingdom of God in prayer have routine habits to consistently pray, so schedule your prayer time with God daily. When you seek first the Kingdom of God and His righteousness, everything will be added unto you (Mathew 6:33).

Abortion is murder, and it defiles and pollutes the land, for the blood of murdered babies cry out for justice and recompense. When Cain killed his brother Abel, a curse was placed upon the land. "And He (God) said, "What have you done? The voice of your brother's blood cries out to Me from the ground. So now you are cursed from the earth, which has opened its mouth to receive your brother's blood from your hand. When you till the ground, it shall no longer yield its strength to you. A fugitive and a vagabond you shall be on the earth." (Genesis 4:10-12). However, through prayer, we can cleanse and heal the land. After

50 years of prayer, Row vs. Wade has been overturned, and the thrones of Baal are being toppled over the nation. Yet, more intercession is required to completely eradicate abortion. "And David built there an altar to the Lord, and offered burnt offerings and peace offerings. So the Lord heeded the prayers for the land, and the plague was withdrawn from Israel" (2 Samuel 24:25). As we remain steadfast, contend for the unborn, and build our altars of prayer, God will heal our land and the plague of abortion will be completely withdrawn from our nation.

As God searches to and fro for those who will partner with Him in prayer, so does creation wait for us to align with Heaven to be brought to earth, for "we know that the whole creation groans and labors with birth pangs together until now" (Romans 8:22) waiting for the children of God—the Ekklesia—to act and take their place in the Kingdom of God.

We are at a critical hour as Dr. Douglas E. Carr illustrates in this powerful book, entitled "Time to Act! The Enemy Snuck in While We Were Sleeping." Yes, we are in a now time to act—to be light and salt in the earth, to be the hands and feet of Jesus to transform our nation and the world. As gross darkness increases in the earth, it is more important than ever that the church pray God's will, God's way for the glory of the Lord to be manifested in all the earth.

Author's Preface

When I entered ministry, I embraced the heresy of false dualism. I wrongly divided my life between sacred and secular. I believed seeking first the Kingdom of God was entirely about leading people to the saving knowledge of Jesus and bringing them into the huddled masses that then gathered on Sunday mornings and evenings, and on Wednesday nights. Yes, we need to bring change to society by leading people to salvation and adding them to the church. But God so loved the WORLD He gave His only begotten son that whosoever believes in Him might not perish but have everlasting life (John 3:16). In the beginning of ministry, my entire focus was the local church.

God's focus is empowering the Ekklesia to bring authentic transformation to the World!

Back then, activities like voting, keeping up on what is going on in society, and addressing societal issues were far less important to me than having good programs to draw more people to attend church.

But God! As I continued studying the Word of God and looking at society through the mirror of the Bible, my eyes were opened to every Christian's commission to be the salt of the earth in every echelon of society.

I began to understand the intent of the Gospel Message and the Great Commission, is not only to affect individuals, but to transform families, education, government, business, arts and media, and every area of community where we are called to bless the cities, we live in.

My intent was to preach a short series, *Suit Up for Battle – The Enemy is at the Door.* Then one morning, during the listening time of my daily devotions, the Lord released the burden of this book when I sensed His leading, as follows.

> I AM giving you *Suit Up for Battle* to be a book to be published before November so it can impact both the midterm and general elections in 2022 and 2024. (For a variety of reasons, I missed that deadline.) The book will go much deeper than the sermons because of their written quality. I will help you revise it as a book that will catch the eyes of many people you do not yet know. Keep it up, Douglas. I am pleased you are brave and will not back down. That is part of your destiny as a reformer. I also want to make you fearless concerning what "might" happen. Continue in the Word and you will see things more clearly than ever before.

My personal intent is to love people to freedom while combatting spiritual powers who have gained traction through human government's refusal to submit to the will and ways of God. God uses godly government to bless people. Satan uses ungodly government to curse people with bondage only Jesus can bring them out of.

📖 Blessed *is* the nation whose God *is* the Lord, the people He has chosen as His own inheritance. Psalm 33:12.

Satan has gained an advantage over the past seventy years as believers and their churches have become increasingly ignorant of what the Bible says.

Solomon was the wisest man ever lived, other than Jesus. He observed the outcome of righteous authority compared to unrighteous.

📖 When the righteous are in authority, the people rejoice; But when a wicked *man* rules, the people groan. Proverbs 28:1.

Our country is a mess and people are groaning because of run-away inflation, surging energy costs, crime in cities and rural areas, including a huge spike in shootings, rioting, thefts, carjackings, and the like.

Let it be known, as we move into the next chapter, my purpose in writing this book is to address spiritual powers and principalities in high places which have brought such a detour in our nation's destiny. Our only hope is to humble ourselves, turn from our wicked ways, and call out to God to save us.

My heart and purpose is to stand with individuals but against promoting unhealthy ideologies.

I stand without compromise against the shedding of innocent blood, sexual perversion of all kinds, and theologies and theories contrary to both the Word of God and the God of the Word.

Chapter One

Why It Matters Now

This call to action was burning in my heart long before I began writing. I mused over it for over weeks, not sure I wanted to face the opposition of humanists and leftists who disagree. I certainly do not want to hurt anyone caught in the deception of this present age.

As I waited on the Lord, I soon knew what I must do. One Monday morning, while I was prayer walking, God told me to begin writing a sermon, "Why Now - Does it Really Matter?"

I sensed the Lord asking, "How many people have given up, and quit trying to make this world a better place?" The thought entered my mind, "God's people know the Great Commission but by in large are not praying or moving forward with the desire to change our communities one person at a time."

Why are believers so lackadaisical concerning the cities, states, and nations they live in? Some don't even bother voting anymore, thinking "what will be will be." Even with the fear of voter fraud, voting is part of our Christian and civic duty. Decisions and appointments to public office are being settled at the ballot box, and those we elect for various offices will appoint people who mirror their own mindsets, as heavenly or hellish as they may be.

I pray for the President's and my state's Governor's appointees every week by name. I've researched them, their views and family, life, marriage, etc. I never remember having as many people appointed to office who have antichrist and unbiblical convictions. We must not remain silent! I'm reminded of an often-quoted statement attributed to Martin Niemöller.

> First, they came for the Socialists, and I did not speak out—Because I was not a Socialist.
>
> Then they came for the Trade Unionists, and I did not speak out—Because I was not a Trade Unionist.
>
> Then they came for the Jews, and I did not speak out—Because I was not a Jew.
>
> Then they came for me—and there was no one left to speak for me.

**It is time to speak out for others before
the devil's henchmen come for us.**

It is very dangerous to think, "that's them, not us." Consider the government overreach during the Covid pandemic. Pastors Che Ahn in California, Rodney

Howard Brown in Florida, and Tony Spell of Louisiana are among many pastors and churches who faced heavy fines and jail time because they chose to obey Hebrews 10:25, and continued meeting after their states joined many others who prosecuted pastors and churches who obeyed the Word of God rather than the injunctions of man.

As I was working on this book on 8/2/22, the State of New York mandated no unvaccinated children would be allowed to attend school! Think of what that will do to their state allowance of thousands of dollars per child. Think what it will do to children and their parents!

It seems like anyone daring to question governmental authority or overreach is rebuked and told to submit to the governing authorities. Paul, who wrote Romans 13, refused to stop preaching the whole Word of God when community leaders resisted him. The early apostles chose to obey God rather than man when told to quit preaching in the name of Jesus.

The Romans 13 passage about submission has everything to do about paying taxes, and nothing to do about attending church!

There is more hope for a fool than there is for anyone who is wise in their own eyes (Proverbs 26:12). Those who build their homes or hopes contrary to the Bible are building them on sand.

I will never forget what some elderly church fathers said on the Sunday following the June 26, 2015, Obergefell v. Hodges decision to made same-sex marriage legal in the United States.

Ed Miller, Dick Bolley, and Dan Hart, who were faithful to Jesus and to our church were unusually despondent that day. Dick launched the discussion when he said, "I never thought I would see the day that America came to this."

They are in heaven now, but I wonder what they might say about the condition America is in now. I believe we are in a darker hour in America than we were in during World War II when Adolf Hitler and his demonized army tried to irradicate Jews and Christians. The lines were clearly drawn between communism and capitalism. The lines are not as clearly drawn now, and the enemy is not nearly as visible—because sometimes the enemy is us!

Therefore, I raise the question, I hope to answer, "Why Now - Does it Really Matter?" It does matter and it is:

Time to Act - The Enemy is at The Door!

Chapter Two

Suit up for Battle! The Enemy is at the Door.

I sense the Lord calling us to address what the Bible says about current hot topics and urge us to suit up for battle because the hour is dark. The enemy is fighting fiercely to not lose any ground gained with Obergefell v. Hodges, the resistance to overturning Roe v. Wade, and WOKE.

**It is time for Believers to know what
the Bible says and why it matters.**

Then, and only then, can we shift our country back to the Christian principles it was founded on. Shortly after I came to Sturgis to pastor in 1992, Pastor Joe Liddick, then pastor of First Wesleyan Church in Sturgis, held the first Pastors' Prayer Summit I ever attended. It was powerful, relational, and inspiring. Joe led a few annual prayer summits before he was transferred to Wheaton. Joe was concerned for Sturgis and every church and every pastor. He even had an associate lead his Sunday evening service so he could attend my commissioning service. Our community suffered great loss when he left.

I tried to keep the Pastors' Prayer Summits going. Unfortunately, they fizzed out after a few years. One pastor told me he didn't like the way I prayed. I asked him why and he said, "because you pray like you believe the devil is real." Surprised, I asked what he thought. He proudly exercised his seminary education, saying, "the devil is only a personification of evil."

I did not argue with him, but Jesus wasn't tempted by a personification of evil in the wilderness. It was not a symbolical being that continued seeking opportune times to attack the Lord (Luke 4:13). One year I looked for the "opportune (kairos – appointed) times" where Satan accused and attacked Jesus. I was surprised at the number of occasions listed in Luke's Gospel. Satan, then as now, primarily used people to launch his attacks.

Jesus' half-brother, James, does not tell us to resist a personification of evil when he says, "resist the devil and he will flee" (James 4:7).

The last time I hosted a Pastors' Prayer Summit, two prominent pastors turned it into a debate because they believed in Universalism, also called "Universal Reconciliation. This deceptive doctrine has caught many people off guard. It teaches all people will go to heaven, even though Jesus Christ said, "unless a person is born again, they will never enter the Kingdom of Heaven" (John 3:3).

📖 Jesus said to him, "I am the way, the truth, and the life. No one comes to the Father except through Me. John 14:6.

One of the proponents of Universalism had been the pastor of a conservative Mennonite Church. When our discussion turned to politics, he said he did not believe in voting because Jesus called His followers out of this world. He believed we had to choose between the Kingdom of God and the kingdoms of this world. I loved the man, now deceased. But his theology was not biblical and too few Christians, including Christian pastors know the Bible well enough to discern between truth and error.

The Commission of the Kingdom of God calls us to transform every segment of Society!

Jesus, in various forms, near the end of each of the four Gospels, commissioned every believer to impact all of society. Each commission is directed more to what Believers are called to do outside the church than what they do within the walls of the buildings, Believers mistakenly call "Church." Jesus called Believers together as an Ekklesia (Greek word often translated "Church" in English) that builds itself up in love, unity, and anointing so it will powerfully impact the communities, states, and nations of the world.

You can probably finish this quote, "And I will tell you that you are Peter, and on this rock, I will build my

_____ and the gates of Hell will not prevail against it" (Matthew 16:18). You were correct if you put the English word "church" in the blank.

Unfortunately, the Greek word "Ekklesia," usually translated in English as "church," has come to mean "us four and no more" who gather in buildings every Sunday to sing songs and listen to sermons that bring little change in us or to the world we live in.

Fourty-two of the Bibles I study regularly translate Ekklesia as "church." Other translations use community (2), assembly (4), congregation (3) and kehillah, My Chavvrah "the community of Moshech."

I like the Message Bible because it gives insight to the mission Jesus gives.

📖 Therefore, Jesus came back, "God bless you, Simon, son of Jonah! You didn't get that answer out of books or from teachers. My Father in heaven, God himself, let you in on this secret of who I really am (and the secret of what we are supposed to do). And now I'm going to tell you who you are, *really* are. You are Peter, a rock. This is the rock on which I will put together my church, a church so expansive with energy that not even the gates of hell will be able to keep it out.
Matthew 16:17–18 MSG.

The Jubilee Bible names and defines Ekklesia as "called out ones," making it the translation closest to a word for word translation from the Greek.

📖 And I say also unto thee, That thou art Peter, *a small rock* and upon the *large* rock I will build my congregation, {Gr. Ekklesia — called out ones} and the gates of Hades shall not prevail against her. Matthew 16:18 Jubilee Bible.

Unfortunately, because we have not been the Ekklesia, the gates of hell have prevailed for the past 50 years.

Ekklesia is well defined in Strongs Greek Concordance #G1577. You can study it by placing the number in your browser. The best way I know to describe it is:

Ekklesia is an assembly called out of the world to be empowered to impact the world.

This book exhorts those calling themselves Believers, to return both to the Word of God and to God of the Word.

Jesus calls us to be salt and light to the world, not pew-sitters, stroking ourselves in the confines of church buildings that may not remain unless, by faith we begin to exercise dominion, power, and authority outside the walls of our sanctuaries.

Do you get what I am saying? This world is headed to hell in a handbasket, and it will not change unless we accept what Jesus exhorts His followers to do when He discussed the ministry of John the Baptist.

John the Baptist was a Kingdom mover and shaker in every realm he walked in.

Both Jesus and John took the Kingdom of God seriously! Their messages touched family, religion, government, business, society, etc.

We think of John as the man who wore skins of camel's hair and feasted on locusts and wild honey (Matthew 3:4). But John the Baptist was a fearless man who called members of every realm of society to repent, for the Kingdom of God is at hand—near—right here with us. It is interesting, John operated by and large outside the synagogues, calling people from every walk of life to step up and walk the life of the King of Kings and Lord and Lords.

We must debunk the false dualism between sacred and secular!

False dualism says what we do on Sundays is sacred and what we do on Mondays is secular. It says going to "church" is sacred but going to work is secular. That is false doctrine. Seeking first the Kingdom of God and His righteousness (Matthew 6:33) is not a Sunday event; seeking first the Kingdom of God is supposed to be every hour, every day, every week, and month endeavor, not relegated to the First Day of the week! Paul reinforces this aspect in his writings.

📖 Therefore, whether you eat or drink, or whatever you do, do all to the glory of God. 1 Corinthians 10:31.

Look around at the average adult attending worship services. It is easy to tell we do not limit our eating and drinking to Sunday mornings. We eat multiple times daily, but God's purpose is to strengthen us, both physically and spiritually via the Word of God, to do His will and advance His Kingdom continually, everywhere we go.

📖 23 And whatever you do, do it heartily, as to the Lord and not to men, 24 knowing that from the Lord you will receive the reward of the inheritance; for you serve the Lord Christ. Colossians 3:23–24.

We cannot serve two masters.
We are soldiers in the Kingdom of God.

📖 "No servant can serve two masters; for either he will hate the one and love the other, or else he will be loyal to the one and despise the other. You cannot serve God and mammon." Luke 16:13.

We fool ourselves when we think Jesus is our master on Sunday morning, but not on Monday morning when we go to work. We are called to serve Jesus as Master at home, church, and work!

The Bible instructs us to work to provide for our families and says we are worse than infidels if we do not provide for them (1 Timothy 5:8).

The Biblical motivation for work includes carrying the presence and glory of God to the places we work and sharing the Good News of Jesus with our fellow employees.

I became a Christian after Dick, a fellow worker at a grocery store found Jesus, and then talked to me about my need for Jesus. He was the first major influencer for Jesus in my life—and he did it as we worked hard together! He did not know the Bible very well, he was not eloquent of speech, but He loved Jesus and me enough to tell me how to be saved.

I confess I was more engaged in soul winning back then, than I am now, partly because I had far more unsaved friends then. I still lead people to Christ in appointments and at jail, but I admit my (our) need for greater compassion for the lost. A primary way of reforming society is leading individuals to the transforming power of Jesus Christ. This leads to a couple of questions.

1) **If God seems far away, guess who moved?**

2) **If the world around you is growing darker, guess who has a job to do?**

Who are you? You are who? Don't be like Moses whose first responses were, "Here I am, send someone else." "Here I am, but I am not up to it." Here I am, but I'm not a good speaker." (Exodus 3:3–14). Don't be like Gideon who made excuses, beginning with, "I am the runt of a runt tribe of a runt nation—you can't be serious about calling me" (Judges 6:11–16).

God is calling us, not because we know it all, but because His calling is our enabling!

Are you tired of inflation, shortages, lying and manipulating politicians who promise great things, and deny we are in recession? Are you tired of politicians and political ads promising much and producing little? What will you do about it? What does God want you to do?

Are you fearful of increasing government intrusion in our schools, businesses, and churches? Do you lack trust in Green New Deal theorists who are so bent on forcing electric cars down our throats that they block energy independence, forcing gas prices out of sight, then forcing them down just before elections?

I learned my lesson as a pastor when I did not stand up to government infringing on the free exercise of religion in 2020. We caved into political pressure to close our church, contrary to Hebrews 10:25, which forbids the forsaking of assembling of ourselves together.

We tried ministering through YouTube, Internet, and mail. We videoed messages, plus I sent a daily devotional to our people via Email. Those devotions turned into a 335-page devotional book, *Light in the Darkness ~ Nuggets of Wisdom Spoken Amidst Trying Times*.

YouTube, Livestreaming, and Emails can never replace the power of people gathering in the Name of Jesus. I soon came under conviction it was wrong for me to give into governmental mandates when God calls us to gather in Jesus' Name. We began holding services again. We practiced caution to prevent the spread of disease, but we still paid a heavy price for the five weeks we closed. In those five weeks, we permanently lost one-third of our congregation. I followed up on those who left for weeks and months and finally had to ask myself the question, "Am I called to babysit backsliders or build an army?"

Some churches refused to close and had cars towed from church parking lots. Brave pastors were thrown into jail, and they and their churches were levied huge fines because they refused to back down from their biblical convictions.

Pam and I ministered at Floodgate Church in Brighton, Michigan in March of 2022. They never closed their doors. They were severely criticized by those driven by media induced fear, but their size has continued to multiply then and since. Their continued growth demanded they expand seating capacity, and they have transformed a bowling alley into a lovely church edifice they moved into in December 2022.

Christian businesses, including one just north of Sturgis, are being fined and/or shut down for staying true to biblical convictions. In 2022, Michigan's Attorney General said she would not enforce LAWS that run contrary to her perverted and rebellious mindset. The days are dark, but light shines brightest in the darkest hours. It is time for Believers to develop biblical mindsets and stand upon the written Word of God. God blesses those who stand on their convictions.

It is very sad when politicians consider themselves to be a law unto themselves.

It is even worse when we allow them to get away with it!

We are concerned! We should be. But part of the problem is those who confess to be Christian do not study the Word of God enough to know what is right and what is wrong in the eyes of God Almighty.

A national survey about the worldview of Americans showed that although 7 out of 10 consider themselves to be Christian, just 6% possess a biblical worldview.

This is tragic, but it explains why many who call themselves Christians, endorse what God says is abomination and celebrate what the Bible says will land people in hell where the worm does not die, and fire is not quenched. Jesus calls for radical change!

📖 43 If your hand causes you to sin, cut it off. It is better for you to enter into life maimed, rather than having two hands, to go to hell, into the fire that shall never be quenched— 44 where 'Their worm does not die and the fire is not quenched.' 45 And if your foot causes you to sin, cut it off. It is better for you to enter life lame, rather than having two feet, to be cast into hell, into the fire that shall never be quenched. Mark 9:43–45.

God the Father, God the Son, and God the Holy Spirit put the Word of God first, even above all their own name.

📖 I will worship toward Your holy temple, and praise Your name for Your lovingkindness and Your truth; for You have magnified Your word above all Your name. Psalm 138:2.

God's Word was held in high esteem in America from its founding. Building on a firm foundation, she prospered. In 1963, the Supreme Court Struck down mandatory readings from the Bible in public schools as unconstitutional. Since then, school violence, bullying, etc. have increased and moral stability has declined. Between 1960 and 1990 divorce doubled, teenage pregnancy went up 200%, teen suicide increased 300%, and violent crime went up 500%.

Ignoring the truth of the Word of God and the power of prayer brings moral decline individually and nationally. Only the proud and blind cannot see the decline our country and schools face. Dare I say, "according to the Solomon and Isaiah, we have many fools leading our country?"

📖 Do you see a man wise in his own eyes? *There is* more hope for a fool than for him. Proverbs 26:12.

📖 Woe to *those who are* wise in their own eyes, and prudent in their own sight! Isaiah 5:21.

We have politicians who think they know more than God Almighty. They refuse to uphold laws prohibiting abortion when God says the shedding of innocent blood pollutes the land. They are in favor of unlimited definitions of marriage, boy-girl, man-woman, man-man, woman-woman, right or wrong, clean and unclean. Some are so foolish they cannot even define words like "woman" or "marriage."

**It will take people of biblical conviction
to bring change to America.**

Isn't it time for those who call themselves Christian to follow Jesus' example and diligently study the Word and present themselves approved to God, workers who do not need to be ashamed, but rightly divide the Word of Truth? (2 Timothy 2:15)

One final point before we close this chapter. It is short and poignant.

Separation of Church and state leaves government to the devil!

Thankfully, Americans, for the most part, still have freedom of religion. They are not bound to a national or state church. The first amendment prohibits the federal government from any involvement in religion. In no way does it ban Believers from speaking to and shaping government to bring it into conformity with God's laws.

God is government! There is no power that exists but for God. Any power that refuses to obey the commandments of the Lord is illegitimate. The government rests upon Jesus' shoulders and of the increase of His government there shall be no end (Isaiah 9:6–7). America's branches of government are founded on Isaiah nine.

📖 For the Lord *is* our Judge, (Judicial Branch)
   The Lord *is* our Lawgiver, (Legislative Branch)
   The Lord *is* our King; (Executive Branch)
   He will save us); Isaiah 33:22. (notes mine)

It is time for the Ekklesia to suit up for battle and do whatever it takes to make the three branches of government in our states and countries line up with their foundation in the Word of God!

Jesus highlights the Kingdom of God and encourages believers to fight to advance His Kingdom. Consider His words from Matthew 11.

📖 11 "Assuredly, I say to you, among those born of women there has not risen one greater than John the Baptist; but he who is least in the kingdom of heaven is greater than he. 12 And from the days of John the Baptist until now the kingdom of heaven suffers violence, and the violent take it by force. Matthew 11:11–12.

It is time to join forces, Be the Ekklesia, and do whatever it takes to advance the Kingdom of God in America.

Chapter Three

War Over the Shedding of Innocent Blood

Let it be known as we begin this chapter: my wife and I love all people. Our desire is to minister unconditional love, acceptance, and forgiveness to everyone. We love people enough to warn them if they are committing sin the Scripture says will land them in hell if they do not repent. We minister freedom, not condemnation, but some biblical truths clearly call for repentance. I must stay true to what the Bible says.

Without repentance, people perish.

I look at the extremes in weather including wildfires, drought, hurricanes, typhoons, tornados, heat waves, flooding, blizzards, etc. and wonder if there is more behind such things than the use of fossil fuels and the carbon footprint we have left. Could there be spiritual things at work too? Believers often quote 2 Chronicles 7:14, especially during prayer events. I've learned a text without a context is a pretext. So, let's look at the larger context.

📖 When I shut up heaven and there is no rain, or command the locusts to devour the land, or send pestilence among My people, [14] if My people who are called by My name will humble themselves, and pray and seek My face, and turn from their wicked ways, then I will hear from heaven, and will forgive their sin and heal their land. [15] Now My eyes will be open and My ears attentive to prayer *made* in this place. 2 Chronicles 7:13–15.

This context shows prayer and repentance are necessary to bring the blessing of God to us individually and nationally. A huge problem with many government programs is they support harmful behaviors rather than empowering people to overcome them. God still calls people, all people, to repentance!

📖 The Lord is not slack concerning *His* promise, as some count slackness, but is longsuffering toward us, not willing that any should perish but that all should come to repentance. 2 Peter 3:9.

Our nation must repent of the sin of abortion. Even though Roe v. Wide was overturned in by the Supreme Court of the United States on June 28, 2022, many antichrist politicians with no regard for the Bible are, as Michigan's Governor Gretchen Witmer says, "fighting like hell to keep abortion safe and legal in the state." Abortion is never safe for a preborn child. No repentance there!

Abortion not only snuffs out the life of an innocent child, but it also causes regret, emotional pain, spiritual and physical issues for the mother.

We have ministered to hundreds of women who had abortions and men who were still involved in the lives of the women they impregnated whose babies were aborted. God knows the name of every child, including those who were not permitted life beyond the womb. We ask parents to name their aborted child if they have not. The day before writing this chapter, we ministered to a dear woman who had never received healing for an abortion she had thirty years previous.

When she asked the Lord her baby's name, He immediately gave her the full name of that precious child. We led her in committing her son to the Lord. She submitted to healing ministry and was set free from burdens she carried for decades.

When both parents of an aborted child are present, I give them a slip of paper and ask them to write the name of the child they aborted. To this date, without conferring with each other, they have always written the same name with the same spelling!

Pastor Stan Dudka has visited heaven in the Spirit several times. One time he met a large group of people who had been aborted. They cried out for him to tell people to name them. I understand and personally believe it is important to assign names to children who have been miscarried or aborted.

Out of the hundreds of post-abortive parents we have ministered to, only one person has ever continued justifying their abortion or been happy about it. The others have struggled with guilt, loss, condemnation, and self-condemnation. Our approach to post abortive parents is akin to Jesus' response to the woman at the well. She ended up becoming the town evangelist.

Jesus did not ignore her sin
but showed her a way out.

My wife and I love ministering healing and deliverance to post abortive parents. We choose to love, accept, and forgive them and lead them to God's love, acceptance, and forgiveness. We want to be like Jesus and treat those who have made some bad choices like Jesus treated the woman the Pharisees caught in the act of adultery.

After leaving the ministry in 1987, the first message I preached in 1990 at a jail and then at a church in White Pigeon, was titled "Mercy is the Most Redemptive."

We cannot influence people toward the Kingdom by
judging them or looking down our noses on them.

This message came out of my own experience. I was so ashamed when I went through a divorce in 1987. I resigned the congregation I loved, and the church and school I help build from the ground up. I never thought anyone would ever love, accept, or forgive me, including God. I thought my days in ministry were over. I visited twenty-six churches in three years, and most of them had little use for a divorced single father with three children. There was one notable exception, a small and loving Baptist Church in a nearby community, but I kept searching for more.

Then I was asked to help lead a Youth for Christ choir. Soon I was asked to preach in a county jail and occasionally at surrounding churches.

My message was developed out of personal need but became central to my ministry. It helps me "hate sin but love sinners." It was based on John 8:1–11. I will expound some on each passage as we look at it.

📖 But Jesus went to the Mount of Olives. ² Now early in the morning He came again into the temple, and all the people came to Him; and He sat down and taught them. ³ Then the scribes and Pharisees brought to Him a woman caught in adultery. And when they had set her in the midst, ⁴ they said to Him, "Teacher, this woman was caught in adultery, in the very act. ⁵ Now Moses, in the law, commanded us that such should be stoned. But what do You say?" John 8:1–5.

Some bibles translate the Greek "de" of the first word of verse one as "and," I prefer the translation "but." People were coming to the temple to listen to Jesus . . .

But the religious people were worried about being right, not loving, and ministering God's grace.

They dragged a humiliated woman into the temple who had been caught committing adultery. These religious hypocrites were bent on shaming the woman, while ignoring her sexual partner altogether. This makes me wonder if they assigned one of their own partners to set the woman up by fornicating with her.

They knew the Scriptures well enough to point their boney fingers at this poor woman, but not enough to know the Lord desires mercy, not sacrifice. They were into judging everyone but themselves and wanted to publicly accuse Jesus of something—anything to make Him look guilty and themselves look better.

📖 [6]This they said, testing Him, that they might have *something* of which to accuse Him. But Jesus stooped down and wrote on the ground with *His* finger, as though He did not hear. [7]So when they continued asking Him, He raised Himself up and said to them, "He who is without sin among you, let him throw a stone at her first." [8]And again He stooped down and wrote on the ground. [9]Then those who heard *it,* being convicted by *their* conscience, went out one by one, beginning with the oldest *even* to the last. John 8:6–9a.

These religious phonies would not let it go. They "repeatedly asked Jesus," until He raised Himself up and spoke His famous words, "He who is without sin among you, let him throw a stone at her first." He never denied the biblical punishment for adultery was stoning. He just demanded they examine themselves before condemning her. The Bible doesn't say what Jesus wrote in the sand, but they became so convicted they went out, beginning with the oldest. I think Jesus was etching their sins in the sand: fornication, pride, hypocrisy, etc. I love what Jesus did next.

Jesus was without sin and could have thrown the first stone, but He chose mercy and grace.

Some people say mercy is God not giving us what we deserve, and grace is God giving us what we do not deserve. I define Grace as the God given desire and power to do God's will, God's way. Jesus perfectly demonstrated mercy and grace.

Religious condemnation cannot release grace, but the mercy of the Lord certainly does!

📖 And Jesus was left alone, and the woman standing in the midst. ¹⁰ When Jesus had raised Himself up and saw no one but the woman, He said to her, "Woman, where are those accusers of yours? Has

no one condemned you?" ¹¹ She said, "No one, Lord." And Jesus said to her, "Neither do I condemn you; go and sin no more."
John 8:9b–11.

**Religious condemnation brings judgement.
Love and forgiveness release healing.**

The focus of this chapter is not condemning post abortive parents, or even those who perform abortions. As much as the Lord and I detest the work of politicians and practitioners who promote abortion, my purpose is to shed biblical light on a controversial subject and spur Believers into action to produce a godlier civilization that honors life.

📖 ⁵ Now the purpose of the commandment is love from a pure heart, *from* a good conscience, and *from* sincere faith, ⁶ from which some, having strayed, have turned aside to idle talk, ⁷ desiring to be teachers of the law, understanding neither what they say nor the things which they affirm.
1 Timothy 1:5–7.

Too many people in pulpits and pews have strayed from the Bible—labeling as good, things God hates.

It is never loving to ignore sin or biblical judgment. Will we choose to love people enough to help them escape sure condemnation? We must not remain silent.

Earlier, I explained God is Government, and the three branches of the United States Government are based on the Word of God.

📖 (For the Lord *is* our Judge, (Judicial Branch)
The Lord *is* our Lawgiver, (Legislative Branch)
The Lord *is* our King; (Executive Branch)
He will save us); Isaiah 33:22.

If we follow God's prototype for government, our countries and communities can be saved. In the Lord's Prayer, Jesus taught us to pray in the imperative: "Kingdom Come! Will be Done! On this earth as it is in heaven!"

As citizens of the United States of America (or other nations) we must stand and fight for God's approved government. The alternative is surrendering to the leadership of officials who are wise in their own eyes. They put themselves above God and legislate contrary to the Word of God. Whose ways do you think are higher, God's or man's?

On June 24, 2022, the United States Supreme Court overturned Roe v. Wade, ending 50 years of federal abortion rights, and thereby turning this decision over to the states.

KEY POINTS

- The Supreme Court in a 5-4 decision overturned Roe v. Wade, the landmark ruling that established the constitutional right to abortion.

- Roe since 1973 had permitted abortions during the first two trimesters of pregnancy in the United States.

- Almost half the states are expected to outlaw or severely restrict abortion as a result of the Supreme Court's decision on a Mississippi case known as Dobbs v. Jackson Women's Health Organization.

- Justice Samuel Alito wrote the majority opinion, joined by three other conservatives. The four liberal justices opposed the decision.

- Chief Justice John Roberts voted with the majority to uphold the Mississippi abortion restrictions but did not approve of tossing out Roe altogether.

Citizens of the Kingdom of God should know God's Ways are Higher.

📖 8 "For My thoughts *are* not your thoughts, nor are your ways My ways," says the Lord. 9 "For *as* the heavens are higher than the earth, so are My ways higher than your ways, And My thoughts than your thoughts. Isaiah 55:8–9.

I realize some people may take offense at this. I challenge them to compare what I say to the Word of God. Recently, I witnessed an angry outburst during a meeting. A woman in a group I am part of, was sharing an excellent article she wrote on personal choice, responsibility, and consequences. One latecomer arrived as the woman said, "Abortion is not birth control, it is murder."

We were shocked by the angry hateful reply from the woman who considers herself a Christian and minister of healing. She disparagingly said, "those are not babies, they are fetuses," implying abortion merely removes unwanted tissue. I truly care for this woman, but it was tense for a while. What happened there was a microcosm of today's society.

A majority of voters in Kansas voted to protect abortion fights in August 2022. Michigan's Attorney General publicly stated she would not enforce the law forbidding abortion. After Roe v. Wade was overturned Michigan's governor joined several other Democrat governors and the Democrat President and his cronies in pledging to protect abortion. They claim to be fighting for women's rights. But they have no sympathy for female and male babies growing within their mother's wombs.

Michigan's Governor Gretchen Whitmer did not realize how accurate she was when she repeatedly stated, "I will fight like hell to protect abortion rights." In my eyes, she was fighting *like* hell and *with* hell to remove protection from unborn babies.

The Bible says there is more hope for a fool than for people who think their opinions trump God's Word.

Supreme Court Justice Samuel Alito said the 1973 Roe ruling and repeated subsequent high court decisions reaffirming Roe "Must be overruled because they were egregiously wrong." By a 5-4 ruling where justices appointed by Republicans voted in favor of overturning Roe and justices appointed by Democrats voted to continue the curse of Roe over America.

Scripture warns against shedding innocent blood.

📖 So you shall not pollute the land where you *are;* for **blood defiles the land**, and no atonement can be made for the land, for the blood that is shed on it, except by the blood of him who shed it. Numbers 35:33. Emphasis mine.

Our state and country's land are defiled by the bloodletting of innocent babies. Consider the following three passages from the Bible, with a few comments following each.

📖 Keep yourself far from a false matter; **do not kill the innocent** and righteous. For I will not justify the wicked. Exodus 23:7. Emphasis mine.

Who can possibly be more innocent than an unborn child or those protecting them?

📖 Their feet run to evil, And **they make haste to shed innocent blood**; Their thoughts *are* thoughts of iniquity; Wasting and destruction *are* in their paths. [8] The way of peace they have not known, and *there is* no justice in their ways; They have made themselves crooked paths; Whoever takes that way shall not know peace. Isaiah 59:7–8. Emphasis mine.

The spiritual powers of darkness do not have physical hands to perform abortions or sign bills protecting, so they influence people to carry out their deadly work.

📖 These six *things* the Lord hates, Yes, seven *are* an abomination to Him: [17] A proud look, A lying tongue, **Hands that shed innocent blood,** [18] A heart that devises wicked plans, Feet that are swift in running to evil, [19] A false witness *who* speaks lies, Proverbs 6:16–19. Emphasis mine.

The left believes the lie "All you need is love." They urge us to just love those who make decisions to end innocent life in the womb. After all, they quip, "God is love." We forget there are things God hates.

God hates the hands of every abortionist. He loves the person enough to sacrifice His Son for their salvation, but He hates what their hands do. They will pay a horrible penalty for their sin if they do not repent. I pray "prochoice politicians, judges, and abortionists" will have nightmares and hear the screams of babies being mutilated in the womb. I hope they will listen to the sorrows of those who have aborted a child. I pray they will repent.

The Shedding of Innocent Blood Pollutes the Land.

Do you ever wonder if God has forsaken America? Has He turned her over to the just penalty of her sin? I believe His grace triumphs still, but we must do everything we can and pray for great repentance and revival in this land. If not, God may forsake our land because of our iniquity.

📖 Then He said to me, "The iniquity of the house of Israel and Judah *is* exceedingly great, and the land is full of **bloodshed**, and the city full of perversity; for **they say, 'The Lord has forsaken the land, and the Lord does not see!'** Ezekiel 9:9. Emphasis mine.

> **The Lord sees, and wants to save, but only righteousness will save a nation.**

Consider the states suffering the greatest harm from tornadoes, wildfires, rioting, murders, violence, school shootings, etc. It appears to me, the more liberal a state is, the more troubles they experience.

📖 Righteousness exalts a nation, But sin *is* a reproach to *any* people. Prov. 14:34.

The Lord has not forsaken this land.
This land has forsaken the One who can save.

📖 [8] You have despised My holy things and profaned My Sabbaths. [9] **In you are men who slander to cause bloodshed**; in you are those who eat on the mountains; in your midst they commit lewdness. Ezekiel 22:8–9. Emphasis mine.

The Lord does judge people and nations who slander and cause bloodshed. Our leaders and nation are found guilty and wanting in this!

📖 [2] *By* swearing and lying, killing and stealing and committing adultery, They break all restraint, **With bloodshed upon bloodshed**. [3] **Therefore the land will mourn**; And everyone who dwells there will waste away With the beasts of the field and the birds of the air; Even the fish of the sea will be taken away. Hosea 4:2–3. Emphasis mine.

I was born in 1951 and have never experienced the depth of mourning America has experienced since the turn of the century.

📖 [4] Hear the word of the Lord, You children of Israel, For the Lord *brings* a charge against the inhabitants of the land: "There is no truth or mercy Or knowledge of God in the land. Hosea 4:1.

Thankfully there is still some truth, mercy, and knowledge of God in the nations of the world. But there is very little truth, mercy, or awareness of God in secular media or political parties that ignore the Word of God.

📖 12 "Woe to him who **builds a town with bloodshed,** Who **establishes a city by iniquity!** 13 Behold, *is it* not of the Lord of hosts That the peoples labor to feed the fire, And nations weary themselves in vain? Habakkuk 2:12–13. ^{Emphasis mine.}

Whole cities, states, and nations have wearied themselves in vain because they have been established on iniquity which builds patterns of perversity which flow through families and groups who refuse to humble themselves and seek God. Consider the words of Jesus . . ..

📖 But Jesus knew their thoughts and said to them: "Every kingdom divided against itself is brought to desolation, and every city or house divided against itself will not stand. Matthew 12:25.

Abortion and sanctity of life is a huge polarizing issue dividing our country. This is an area where we must steer our nation back to what the Bible says.

Anyone who respects God and His Word, knows life begins in the womb.

Unfortunately, there is a large and vocal schism in America that either ignores God and the Bible completely or thinks it knows better than God.

📖 Do you see a man wise in his own eyes? *There is* more hope for a fool than for him. Proverbs 26:12.

Many states and nations are being run by people who are wise in their own eyes and choose personal preference over Bible-based conviction.

Proponents of abortion have their foolish hearts darkened to the point they think a baby growing within a womb is a blob of cells—a fetus—not a person.

The Bible is clear, life begins at conception!

The Lord told Jeremiah He knew him even before he was formed in the womb. Prior to conception, God ordained his destiny.

📖 "Before I formed you in the womb I knew you; Before you were born I sanctified you; I ordained you a prophet to the nations." Jeremiah 1:5.

King David, a man after God's own heart, wrote many of the Psalms. In Psalm 139 he writes how intimately he is involved with each child.

📖 13 For You formed my inward parts; You covered me in my mother's womb. 14 I will praise You, for I am fearfully *and* wonderfully made; Marvelous are Your works, And *that* my soul knows very well. 15My frame was not hidden from You, When I was made in secret, *And* skillfully wrought in the lowest parts of the earth. 16 Your eyes saw my substance, being yet unformed. And in Your book they all were written, The days fashioned for me, When *as yet there were* none of them. [17] How precious also are Your thoughts to me, O God! How great is the sum of them! Psalm 139:13–17.

The Bible is clear; God is intricately involved with the conception and development of every child, beginning at the point of conception.

Each child's destiny is launched within its mother's womb!

This is an incredible thought! God knows His plans to prosper each child as the child grows within the womb! He knows His plans to prosper each boy and girl and not harm them but give them a hope and a future (Jeremiah 29:11–12).

Every abortion kills more than a baby. It also destroys what God intends to do through His handiwork in each child God created on purpose for a purpose!

Could it be the reason it is so difficult to find good presidents, preachers, congressmen, governors, and the like is that many whom God destined to be the George Washingtons, Charles Finney's, Aimee Semple McPhersons, Ronald Reagans, etc. of our day were snuffed out through abortion before they had a chance to serve Jesus?

A parent's job description is to discern what God created each child to do and help them prepare to enter and succeed within his or her prophetic destiny (Ephesians 1:10).

I already had a son when I became a Christian. By the time I took my first church, I had two sons and a daughter. Unfortunately, I was taught that "train up a child in the way he should go" meant turning them into perfect "church kids," or in my case, "preacher's kids."

It didn't take long however, to see how many sincere and loving Christian parents have children who go grossly astray. These parents took their children to church, told them to read their Bibles, and perhaps did daily devotions with them, but they still fell away from the Lord and His Church.

One urgent topic in Christian gatherings is intense prayers for prodigal children to return to the Lord. Could it be we misunderstood the promise of Proverbs 22:6. Look at it from a couple of translations.

📖 Train up a child in the way he should go, And when he is old he will not depart from it. Proverbs 22:6 NKJV.

📖 Train up the child according to the tenor of his way, and when he is old he will not depart from it. Proverbs 22:6 Darby.

📖 Train a child in the way appropriate for him, and when he becomes older, he will not turn from it. Proverbs 22:6 International Standard Bible.

Allow me to wax eloquent here for a moment. Passages like Jeremiah 1:7, Psalm 139, Ephesians 6:10, etc., all speak of God's design for every individual.

God's intentional forming of each child is on purpose for specific purposes.

It is possible the reason employers have trouble finding faithful workers, and restaurants can't find enough employees to keep their restaurants open is those destined to serve the public these ways were snuffed out before they could serve Jesus by serving others. I think so.

📖 [10] For we are His workmanship, created in Christ Jesus for good works, which God prepared beforehand that we should walk in them. Ephesians 2:10.

Abortion kills God's Redemptive Purpose in and through children who are slaughtered.

Before the 2020 presidential election, I talked with professing Christians who were voting Democrat because they thought Joe Biden was nicer than Donald Trump. No amount of persuading would convince them God is displeased when we vote for people who support abortion. Putting a child to death IS destroying God's purpose and destiny for every child.

I write this book out of my concern for the state I live in (Michigan) and the nation I love (U.S.A.). I believe it applies, however, to people in every state and nation. Therefore, I ask a generic question.

Is your state and country rejoicing or groaning?

📖 When the righteous are in authority, the people rejoice; But when a wicked *man* rules, the people groan. Proverbs 29:2.

As I write this chapter in late summer of 2022, my fellow citizens are groaning at the grocery stores and gas stations. Farmers and truckers dependent upon Diesel fuel are groaning. People trying to rear a family or buy their own home are groaning. People who have a biblical worldview groan at sending their children to public schools because of evil their children may be exposed to.

I realize Romans 3:10 says "There is none righteous, no, not one." But God offered a remedy.

When people exercise faith to make Jesus their Lord and Savior, God inputs His righteousness to them.

When they submit fully to Jesus and the Kingdom of God, they are used to reshape nations.

The biblical view of life states shedding innocent blood brings a curse on the land. The same holds true when the biblical view of marriage is ignored, as seen in the next chapter.

Chapter Four

The War for Biblical Marriage

A great war in the heavenlies is being played out on earth. Jehovah and the way of holiness is being assaulted by Satan and the Kingdom of darkness. The devil, his principalities, and powers are working through politicians who are blinded to the way of holiness. Together, they are hellbent on destroying God's purpose for covenant family.

Family is the basic unit of society, which God created as one man, one woman, and the children and generations who follow. Blessings are passed down 1,000 generations to those who love the Lord and obey His commandments. Curses are passed down 4–10 generations of those who rebel against the Lord.

If Satan can destroy the family unit, he will be successful at destroying society at large. He is fully aware of this. Therefore, traditional family, as designed by God, is being fiercely attacked. When I was working on this book in August of 2022, the United States House of Representatives passed H.R. 8404. It is horrible and perverse in the eyes of God!

There has never been a time like now. The people of God need to seek first the Kingdom of God and His righteousness! (Matthew 6:33) Believers must put on their spiritual armor, stand, vote, pray, speak up, and be the light of the world and the salt of the earth. Now is when we need to share the Good News of Jesus!

Satan has built an army of rich and influential people whom he has deceived.

This army is militantly involved in politics, government, family, education, business, media, entertainment, and even in church. Veils cloud the eyes of many, making them blind to God's holiness.

They have no moral standards by which to discern between good and evil.

📖 [20] Woe to those who call evil good, and good evil; Who put darkness for light, and light for darkness; Who put bitter for sweet, and sweet for bitter! [21] Woe to *those who are* wise in their own eyes, And prudent in their own sight! Isaiah 5:20-21.

Foolish people build their houses on sand and when the flood of mortal ills come, their houses will crash. A home or nation built on the rock will stand (Matthew 7:24–27, Luke 6:47–49). God has a remnant building its house on the rock. But the devil is hellbent in manipulating people to build houses of cards in the kingdom of darkness. It is urgent for Believers to grasp what the Bible says and build their homes and lives on the solid Rock of Jesus Christ and the whole counsel of God, given in the Scriptures. We must speak Kingdom Life into America.

One major attack is against God's design for family.

God designed marriage the way He knows is best. He recognized it was not good for man to be alone and created Eve from Adam's rib. Throughout the history of humanity, the design for marriage has been one man and one woman who covenant to love and cherish each other until death they do part. Godly children are the fruit of such unions, as is godly society. Satan wants no part of God's design.

New Life Worship has a wonderful song, Counting on God by Integrity music. The beginning stanza is *I'm in a fight not physical, And I'm in a war. But not with this world. You are the light that's beautiful, And I want more, I want all that's Yours.*

Can we say, "we want all that's God's?" Not if we allow a fringe group to redefine marriage and teach our children "love is love," or "love is all there is," implying biblical standards are obsolete!

We must suit up for battle! The enemy is at the door, trying to destroy marriage as we know it.

📖 We're not waging war against enemies of flesh and blood alone. No, this fight is against tyrants, against authorities, against *supernatural* powers *and demon princes that slither* in the darkness of this world, and against wicked *spiritual armies* that lurk about in heavenly places. Ephesians 6:12 The Voice.

One way this battle is played out is through H.R. 8404.

On July 18, 2022, Jerrold Nadler, Democrat Sponsor Representative for New York's 10th congressional district, sponsored H.R. 8404. In summary it said, "Respect for Marriage Act."

What a farce! It sounds pretty, but it is antichrist, anti-Bible, and anti-family! It disrespects marriage as God created it. This bill provides statutory authority for same sex (and interracial marriages). I have no problem with heterosexual interracial marriages. But same sex marriage is an abomination to God!

Specifically, the bill repeals and replaces provisions that define, for purposes of federal law, marriage as between a man and a woman and spouse as a person of the opposite sex with provisions that recognize any marriage that is valid under state law.

The bill also repeals and replaces provisions that do not require states to recognize same-sex marriages from other states with provisions that prohibit the denial of full faith and credit or any right or claim relating to out-of-state marriages on the basis of sex, race, ethnicity, or national origin. The bill allows the Department of Justice to bring a civil action and establishes a private right of action for violations.

Stories of religious discrimination against bakeries, wedding venues, churches, orchards, candy makers, etc. abound. They are being sued because they stand on their convictions, believing they are guaranteed freedom of religion in the United States.

On July 27, 2022, Senator Lankford (R Okla.) announced he would vote against this bill, marketed as "Respect for Marriage Act." He said it removes all protections from marriage. The legislation which the Senate could consider shortly, imposes a top-down mandate for every state to recognize **any "marriage between two individuals**."

That included time-bound marriages, open marriages, marriages involving a minor or relative, platonic marriages, or any other new marriage definition a state chooses to adopt.

Family research Council's Tony Perkins said if the senate passes this bill, "In all likelihood, this bill will then come straight at every nonprofit that believes in traditional marriage, biblical marriages, etc.'

We have an example eight miles north of our church. Rouch World Amusement Park, Sturgis, Michigan lost their appeal in July 2022.

The Christians who own and run this business, a few miles north of Sturgis, have Bible based convictions. They are not being mean. They are not calling anyone names. They simply would not host a Gay wedding reception. There are plenty of other venues willing to host such a reception, but evidently the state of Michigan does not believe they have a right to choose whom to serve.

The powers of hell are here in force, trying to make the point that a person's opinion trumps God's law.

Therefore, people who refuse to comprise their conviction to cater to what conscience does not allow them to, are up for a fight. So, the state stepped in. The Michigan Supreme Court bypassed the appellate court in agreeing to a Department of Civil Rights request to hear its appeal of a lower-court ruling that held the sex classification in the Elliott-Larsen Civil Rights Act does not encompass sexual orientation.

An order dated Friday, July 2, 2022, and released Saturday in Rouch World LLC v. Department of Civil Rights was the first time the new Democratic majority on the court aligned decisively, with a 4-3 party-line majority on whether to bypass the Court of Appeals and hear the appeal directly from the Court of Claims.

Rouch World is a 300-acre park and wedding venue in Sturgis, according to the company's website. Its owners declined to host a same-sex wedding ceremony because of their religious beliefs.

They filed a lawsuit against the Michigan Department of Civil Rights, arguing the state's Elliott-Larsen Civil Rights Act doesn't protect people from discrimination based on sexual orientation or gender identity.

The Supreme Court's recent decision sets up a potentially landmark ruling that could fulfill the long-sought effort by LGBTQ people and supporters to extend the civil rights protections in the law to people who are gay, lesbian, bisexual or transgender. A December ruling from the Court of Claims held the act applies to gender identity, thus extending protections to transgender persons, but Judge Christopher Murray ruled the word "sex" did not cover discrimination based on someone's sexual orientation.

The Supreme Court called for briefs to be filed within three months, with no extensions unless good cause was shown. The court also said oral arguments would take place with 20 minutes for each side.

The order also invited the following groups to file amicus briefs: The American Civil Liberties Union of Michigan, the American Civil Liberties Union, Affirmations LGBTQ+ Community Center, Equality Michigan, Freedom for All Americans, Human Rights Campaign, LGBT Detroit, National Center for Lesbian Rights, OutCenter of Southwest Michigan, OutFront

Kalamazoo, Ruth Ellis Center, Southern Poverty Law Center, Stand With Trans and Trans Sistas of Color Project. It said other groups or persons may seek permission to file amicus briefs. Please note, no conservative group was invited to file.

In the majority were Chief Justice Bridget McCormack, Justice Richard Bernstein, Justice Megan Cavanagh, and Justice Elizabeth Welch, all of Michigan.

Justice Elizabeth Clement dissented, citing the court's rationale last year for denying bypass in the lawsuit against Gov. Gretchen Whitmer's use of the Emergency Powers of the Governor Act to keep Michigan under a state of emergency.

This may be boring, but we need to hear and understand the enemy's schemes.

"This was in the face of the fact that the case raised compelling questions that implicated the civil liberties of all Michiganders—just as this one does. We should deny this bypass application just like we denied that one," Clement wrote.

Clement said, "just as was the case in the pandemic powers case, the department cannot show any substantial harm it would receive as a result of going through the ordinary appellate process."

The battle lines are drawn, and the left is armed and hovering at the line. Where is the Ekklesia??

God is not against any human. He truly wants everyone to be saved and live godly lives.

📕 The Lord is not slack concerning *His* promise, as some count slackness, but is longsuffering toward us, not willing that any should perish but that all should come to repentance. 2 Peter 3:9.

Repentance is an unequivocal condition of salvation and transformation. God will save anybody, no matter how wicked, IF they repent.

There is a big bad wolf huffing and puffing at the door of American decency. Our houses will not stand if we build them of straw or sticks. We have a roaring, devouring loin prowling, seeking whom he may devour (1 Peter 5:8).

Little Red Riding Hood describes a big bad wolf sees the basket of goodies a little girl is carrying to refresh her sick grandma. He runs ahead, and gobbles grandma whole, then disguises himself as Grandma. When the girl arrives, she notices her grandmother looks very strange. She says, "What a deep voice you have!" ("The better to greet you with," responds the wolf), "Goodness, what big eyes you have!" ("The better to see you with," responds the wolf), "And what big hands you have!" ("The better to embrace you with", says the wolf), and lastly, "What a big mouth you have" ("The better to eat you with!" responds the wolf). The wolf jumped up and swallowed his victim.

Thankfully, a wood cutter comes to the rescue with an axe and cuts open the sleeping wolf. Little Red Riding Hood and her grandmother emerge shaken, but unharmed.

Society has been listening to the big bad wolf far too long. Thankfully, a cross bearer came to save the day! All who look upon Him will live. Then He calls us to join Him, take up our crosses, deny ourselves daily, and truly follow Him (Matthew 16:24).

As I take up my cross, I am compelled to tell the truth about what God says concerning same gender sex and marriage. We do not want gender confusion and marital perversion to bring the curse on America that led to the destruction of Sodom and Gomorrah. Do we?

When examining the Bible's truth about homosexuality, we must distinguish between homosexual behavior and homosexual attractions.

Homosexual behavior and homosexual attraction is the difference between active sin leading to judgment and the passive condition of being tempted.

Homosexual behavior is sinful, but the Bible never says it is a sin to be tempted. Simply stated, a struggle with temptation may lead to sin, but the struggle itself is not sin.

God is love, which is why He opposes same gender marriage.

God, who designed marriage between a man and a woman, designed it so because it is good. Going against God's blessing of traditional marriage brings harm to those who sin against God, themselves, and their partners. For the good of people, God wants perversion removed from people and communities.

📖 And he banished the perverted persons from the land and removed all the idols that his fathers had made. 1 Kings 15:12. (Hebrew *qedeshim*, those practicing sodomy and prostitution in religious rituals.)

The old lie, "If you love me, you will lay with me" is straight from the pit of hell!

Homosexual behavior defiles a nation.

📖 ²² You shall not lie with a male as with a woman. It *is* an abomination. ²³ Nor shall you mate with any animal, to defile yourself with it. Nor shall any woman stand before an animal to mate with it. It *is* perversion. ²⁴ '**Do not defile yourselves** with any of these things; for **by all these the NATIONS are defiled**, which I am casting out before you. Leviticus 18:22–24. Emphasis mine.

God clearly calls same gender sex an abomination, leading to death.

📖 If a man lies with a male as he lies with a woman, both of them have committed an abomination.

They shall surely be put to death. Their blood *shall be* upon them. Leviticus 20:13.

Though capital punishment for deviant sexual behavior does not exist in most civilized societies; Aids, Monkeypox, Syphilis, and many other diseases target a very high percentage of homosexuals, often leading to their early deaths. CNBC reported on August 4, 2002, the Centers for Disease Control and Prevention (CDC) estimates 1.7 million gay and bisexual men face highest risk from monkeypox.

Traditional marriage is God's plan from the beginning and forever.

📖 [6] But from the beginning of the creation, God 'made them male and female.' [7] 'For this reason a man shall leave his father and mother and be joined to his wife, [8] and the two shall become one flesh'; so then they are no longer two, but one flesh. [9]Therefore what God has joined together, let not man separate. Mark 10:6–9.

One of God's greatest blessings is traditional marriage. Jesus came so we might have life more abundantly. Christian marriage is part of God's plan for abundance! The devil comes only to steal, kill, and destroy (John 10:10). Same gender sin is one of Satan's tools of destruction. We must stand for truth against the lies of the devil.

God sadly gives people over to their passions — knowing they might destroy themselves.

Like the prodigal son's father, God will release people to do want they want to, even when He knows the end thereof is destruction. Romans chapter one clearly states God will give people over to their depraved ways if they resist Him and His Word.

📖 26 For this reason God gave them up to vile passions. For even their women exchanged the natural use for what is against nature. 27Likewise also the men, leaving the natural use of the woman, burned in their lust for one another, men with men committing what is shameful, and receiving in themselves the penalty of their error which was due. Romans 1:26–27.

Continued Resistance to God's will brings reprobation.

The word reprobate is used 7 times in the King James Version.

📖 And even as they did not like to retain God in their knowledge, God gave them over to a reprobate mind, to do those things which are not convenient. Romans 1:28 KJV.

I've sat and talked with many parents who were devastated by their child's behavior. They know there isn't much they can do to help a child when the child is determined to continue in detrimental behavior. This must be how God feels when he gives people over to reprobate behavior.

📖 Examine yourselves, whether ye be in the faith; prove your own selves. Know ye not your own selves, how that Jesus Christ is in you, except ye be reprobates? 2 Corinthians 13:5 KJV.

One of the best things we can do for people who are given to reprobate behavior is pray they will examine themselves and see what their behaviors are doing to them and what their end will be if they do not change.

📖 Now as Jannes and Jambres withstood Moses, so do these also resist the truth: men of corrupt minds, reprobate concerning the faith. 2 Timothy 3:8.

Political and governmental resistance to the truth is at an all-time high in our country. A well-known preacher of the 1970's used to say, "If God doesn't judge America soon, He will have to apologize to Sodom and Gomorrah." I remind you here,

I am addressing ideologies, not individuals, for I want America to escape the wrath of God.

Barak Obama publicly stated he did not believe America is a Christian Country. It seems we have a host of spiritual and human enemies bent on making that true.

📖 They profess that they know God; but in works they deny him, being abominable, and disobedient, and unto every good work reprobate. Titus 1:6.

The Greek word "adokimon" is translated "reprobate" in the KJV and "depraved" in many other translations. Strong's Concordance describes it as "unapproved, rejected, worthless, castaway, and reprobate."

Reprobate describes all thinking, talking, living, and voting contrary to God's Word.

By this description, many who lead our state and country are reprobate in God's eyes. I beseech thee, brothers, and sisters, to never again vote for reprobates who rule contrary to the Word of God concerning life in the womb, abortion, marriage, and human sexuality.

It is never loving to steer people from God's truth.

God gave the rainbow as a sign of covenant promise not to destroy the earth again by flood. Even this good symbol has been robbed of its promise, by promising life to those headed to damnation if they do not repent!

Back to Rouch World. July 28, 2022 **DETROIT**–Today, the Human Rights Campaign (HRC)—the nation's largest lesbian, gay, bisexual, transgender and queer (LGBTQ+) civil rights organization—applauds the Michigan Supreme Court for ruling, in a 5-2 opinion, that the state's nondiscrimination law, which prohibits discrimination on the basis of sex, includes sexual orientation. The court's analysis also supported a lower court's opinion that the law prohibits discrimination on the basis of gender identity.

Pastors will be asked to perform same sex weddings! The enemy is at the door. We must not surrender. This is a call to war for decency and life before and after birth. America's young people, especially those trained in government schools and colleges, have been brainwashed into thinking it is loving and kind to support people, regardless of biblical norms, and let them love whomever and whatever they want to love. But the question begs to be asked, is it loving to stand idly by as people choose decadent behaviors the Bible says will land them in the lake of fire?

These matters can sentence people to hell!

📖 ⁵ But I want to remind you, though you once knew this, that the Lord, having saved the people out of the land of Egypt, afterward destroyed those who did not believe. ⁶ And the angels who did not keep their proper domain, but left their own abode, He has reserved in everlasting chains under darkness for the judgment of the great day; ⁷ as Sodom and Gomorrah, and the cities around them in a similar manner to these, **having given themselves over to sexual immorality and gone after strange flesh, are set forth as an example, suffering the vengeance of eternal fire.** Jude 1:5–7. Emphasis mine.

How can anyone in their right mind want eternal judgment for people living in condemning sin? The Bible lists specific ongoing behaviors that bring condemnation.

📖 7 He who overcomes shall inherit all things, and I will be his God and he shall be My son. 8 But the **cowardly**, unbelieving, **abominable**, **murderers, sexually immoral**, sorcerers, idolaters, and all liars shall have their part in the lake which burns with fire and brimstone, which is the second death." Revelation 21:7–8. Emphasis mine.

Could the "cowardly" include people who are fearful of losing nonprofit status if they speak boldly concerning the sin threatening our society?

📖 9 Do you not know that the unrighteous will not inherit the kingdom of God? Do not be deceived. Neither fornicators, nor idolaters, nor adulterers, nor homosexuals, nor sodomites, 10 nor thieves, nor covetous, nor drunkards, nor revilers, nor extortioners **will inherit the kingdom of God**. 11And **such were some of you.** But you were washed, but you were sanctified, but you were justified in the name of the Lord Jesus and by the Spirit of our God. 1 Corinthians 6:9–11. Emphasis mine.

God said it, I believe it, and that is good enough for me—and for every city, state, and nation.

Remember the account of Sodom and Gomorrah? (Genesis 18:1-19:38) God judged them because they were mired in deviant behavior. Abraham interceded for them, asking God not to destroy them. He bargained with the Lord until God said He would not destroy Sodom and Gomorrah if only ten righteous people could be found there. Perhaps Abraham was counting Lot, his wife, his two married daughters and their husbands, along with his two unmarried daughters and their fiancé's. Unfortunately, most of them remained in Sodom and perished, leaving only Lot and his unmarried daughters after the destruction of the city (Reference Gen. Rabbah 50:9; Pirkei de-Rabbi Eliezer, ed. Higger chap. 25).

Sadly, those who escaped the fire and brimstone, did not escape the influence of an ungodly society.

Lot and his daughters left Sodom, but Sodom did not leave them. Lot lost his wife when God destroyed Sodom and Gomorrah. His younger daughter's fiancés likewise perished. Even though they finally took a stand and fled the wickedness of the land, they lost loved ones and ended up in drunkenness and incestuous relations from which were birthed two of Israel's greatest foes, the Moabites and Ammonites.

The battle in America is over the same perversion that destroyed Sodom and Gomorrah and brought heartache to the few people who fled for their lives.

This perversion caused Lot and his remaining daughters to become so morally loose they ended up creating enemies from their own family line.

Wake up. Wake up! We must not compromise. The enemy is at the door. He is alive and well in the White House and many state houses. It is time to stand up, speak up, pray up, and vote righteously. May God use us in saving our state and nation!

Prayer:

✝ In the Name and through the blood of Jesus, we break the curse and iniquitous pattern of wrongful shedding of blood.
✝ We break the curse and iniquitous pattern of abomination of WOKE and heterosexual and homosexual fornication.
✝ We release love and courage to take a righteous stand for America.
✝ So be it, in Jesus' Name. Amen.

Chapter Five

WOKE or Wake Up?

A second grader from our church recently came home from school and said, "My teacher says it is OK for men to marry men and women to marry women." Thankfully, she shared this with godly grandparents who know, believe, and stand on the Word of God! They rightly replied, "That is not what God says," and then shared with her a healthy biblical world view.

How do you feel about young people being taught by their teachers that boys and girls can change gender if they want to? Does it bother you when politicians, teachers and school boards say it is ok for men to marry men and girls to marry girls? Are you concerned children are encouraged to change their gender apart from parental consent?

I think of the man who was appointed Secretary of Health and Human Services in March of 2021. He is a nonmedical person who is pro gender reversal and abortion. I suspect he was chosen because he is a proponent of gender reversal and abortion. I fear the United States has lost its sense of value and decency.

Society has ignored the Word of God
and is becoming increasingly WOKE.

People, from the White House to the Church House to the outhouse, expound values contrary to the Bible. Some Mainline denominations endorse practices the Bible warns will lead straight to hell.

WOKE has gained popularity amid an increasing leftward turn on various issues, mostly among the American left, and partly as a reaction to what Wikipedia calls the right-wing politics of U.S. President Donald Trump.

WOKE endorses Black Lives Matter
and Critical Race Theory.

Black lives do matter. All lives matter. Yellow, black or white, born, and unborn, are precious in God's sight. But WOKE blames everything wrong in the United States of America on its participation in slave trade before the Emancipation Proclamation was issued on January 1, 1863, over 160 years ago. I have participated in identificational repentance concerning our country's sins against African American and Native American people. The Ekklesia has not ignored the nation's sin in the past but has addressed it.

Jesus wants to turn people from their pasts
into His plans for a hope and future.

God wants us to confess and repent of our sins, as well as the sins of our forefathers. He wants us to learn from our past and build stronger foundations in society.

WOKE holds people captive to the past. therefore, promoting ongoing racism.

WOKE includes rejection of American democracy, claiming America has never been a true democracy. Though prejudice still exists, equality among races and people groups were greatly improving before the spread of WOKE ideologies.

WOKE claims people of color suffer systemic and institutional racism, whereas white Americans experience white privilege. African Americans deserve reparations for slavery and post enslavement discrimination, whereas disparities among racial groups, for instance in certain professions or industries, are automatic evidence of discrimination; that U.S. law enforcement agencies are designed to discriminate against people of color and so should be defunded, disbanded, or heavily reformed. WOKE teaches that women suffer systemic sexism, especially if their so-called right to abortion is challenged.

A key WOKE idea is individuals should be able to identify with any gender or none.

The infiltration of WOKE ideology endangers the right to privacy among school children in restrooms and locker rooms. How many children need to be exposed to indecency and rape before the foolishness of men in women bathrooms is rejected? How many women athletes must compete with biological males?

WOKE argues U.S. capitalism is deeply flawed and must be dismantled. Newscasts of widespread rioting and destroying statues that represent our history give evidence WOKE causes more problems than it solves. Social media is increasingly blocking conservative and Christian views.

WOKE fights to control the mindset of Americans with ideologies rejecting the Bible and History.

Anyone with the stomach to listen to the news or watch television will hear lies spouted by mainstream media, secularized newscasts, and daily programming. Secular media is being used to brainwash our nation in WOKE ideology.

Advertising is increasingly designed to make WOKE values acceptable, including same gender marriage, abortion, promiscuity, and other things that are a stench in God's nostrils. Media is reactionary in what it wrongly perceives to be truth.

When a policeman is placed in the horrible split second need to fire a weapon to save lives, WOKE reporting never reports the crime the true villain is committing. Do you think defunding the police helps? Even some on the left are recognizing this error and recanting such lunacy. They have witnessed how unpoliced cities become violent, destructive, and deadly.

In August 2022, Joe Biden was "limited" by sensible members of congress in the amount he could "forgive individual student loans." 87% of this is paid by Americans who have no student loans. This teaches irresponsibility! The Bible says the WICKED do not pay their debts.

The wicked borrows and do not repay,
but the righteous shows mercy and gives. Psalm 37:21

I am grateful part of my college education was learning how to pay for my education, including paying off my student loans in full. I was taught how to handle money because I was held responsible for my debts. Praise God! That is how it should be!

Open our eyes, Lord, to see what is really going on! We have an enemy who is not always visible. The powers and principalities of hell are gaining advantage in suppressing righteousness and advancing wickedness that causes humans and humanity to fall short of the glory of God.

Satan has a powerful army of well-trained demons
and principalities trying to displace the Ekklesia.

Citizens under the control of Satan's army fight to make America a non-Christian nation, militantly using same-gender confusion, abortion, and rebellion to exalt Satan and his kingdom in America. Baal has a foothold in the land I love and respect.

The devil is successfully confusing people concerning gender and sexuality.

We use a thorough questionnaire for deep healing and deliverance appointments. Question 92 asks, "Were you born the right sex?" it gives multiple answers: "Yes, No, and Unsure." Very few answer "No," but the number who respond "Unsure" is surprising.

"Unsure" is often selected by children whose parent or parents wanted them to be the opposite gender than they are. For one reason or another, one or both parents wanted the child to be the opposite gender than their God-given gender.

The "unsure" answer is also chosen by people who were molested as children. In both cases, the devil is at work trying to make them reject their God-given gender. Healing usually comes as we minister deep healing from conception.

During this process, we ask God to open their Book of Remembrance (Malachi 3:16). God pays so much attention to each person; He has a book of remembrance containing every detail of every person's life. In deep healing from conception, we begin with the egg and seed that came together when they were conceived. When their gender becomes apparent as we lead them through each month in the womb, we ask them how Jesus responds to their gender. He always responds with a life-giving affirmation of heaven's joy that they were designed to be the gender they were born with. Jesus usually reinforces their gender with a warm and loving smile, reflecting God's pleasure they were created male or female. (I explain this process in my book *Holy Spirit as Counselor ~ Partnering with God in Healing.)*

> **The devil realizes if he can control a person's thinking, he can control the person, for as a a man thinks in his heart, so is he (Proverbs 23:7).**

Jesus said the thief comes to kill, steal, and destroy (John 10:10). Woke-ism is a theory and mindset straight out of the gates of hell, designed to bring death and destruction to everyone who falls for it. For example, a 2007 paper showed about 25% of transgender youth had attempted suicide at least once. Is that what we want for our sons, daughters, and grandchildren? Is it what we want America? Wake up, Ekklesia! We are in a battle we cannot afford to lose. God forbid we lose it for the sake of our grandchildren!

If the devil can confuse a female into thinking she is male, or a male into thinking he is or wants to be a female, she or he will begin adopting a perverted self-image, contrary to heaven's design for the person.

WOKE politicians, blind to the ways of God, put woman athletes at a disadvantage as they give wanna be women the advantage, because they were given male bodies by God Almighty. The thought school children can be given gender transitioning drugs without parental knowledge or permission is chilling. Such people, who are wise in their own eyes, are fools. They never admit the damage caused by tampering with God given gender. Let me name a few:

Side effects and Risks of Gender Reassignment Surgery. Some of the risks of the gender reassignment procedure are due to the hormone therapy itself. These include:

- High blood pressure,
- Sleep apnea,
- Heart disease,
- Tumors affecting the pituitary gland,
- Infertility,
- Uncontrolled weight gain,
- High levels of liver enzymes,
- Blood clots,
- Anxiety, and
- Feelings of uncertainty and confusion.[1]

[1]Irainiansurgery.com: Side Effects and Risks of Gender Reassignment Surgery.

We need to repent, turn back to a Biblical Worldview, and campaign for biblical values.

Chapter Six

Amendment to Title IX

My eyes were opened to this threat on August 24, 2022. Dutch Sheet's Daily Give Him 15 title was, *One of the Most Egregious Governmental Actions Yet.* He wanted Americans to be aware of Joe Biden's attempt to expand Title IX. Dutch said this is "one of the largest, most aggressive social engineering overreaches of the government in America's history."

I have given what he shared a lot of thought and did my part in submitting my objections to it.

This is nothing less than a federally mandated indoctrination of our children.

Vernadette Broyles of Child and Parental Rights Campaign, said this regulation "will directly affect 77 million children, requiring the normalization and unquestioned acceptance of gender identity ideology as part of their school environment. The threat to parental rights, children's physical, mental, and spiritual well-being, religious liberties, freedom of speech, girls' safety and sports, and more is potentially devastating."2 http:childparentrights.org/tithe-IX/

Title IX of the Education Amendments was enacted by Congress in 1972 to eliminate discrimination in education based upon sex (gender), against girls and women in particular.3 Neal v BD. Of Trs. Of Cal. State University, 198.

It states: No person in the United States shall, on the basis of sex (gender), be excluded from participation in, be denied the benefits of, or be subjected to discrimination under any education program or activity receiving Federal financial assistance . . . 420 U.S.C. 1681A.

When Title IX was passed, girls and women faced high barriers to pursuing educational opportunities, particularly in higher education.5 North Haven bod of Educ. V. Bell, 3456 U.S 512.526-27 (1982)

Title IX was designed to remove those barriers and represents 50 years of progress in education made by girls and women.

Title IX regulates every public K-12 school, college, and university in the nation, as well as every private school that takes federal funding. As a result, it has wide-reaching implications for tens of millions of children and parents across the country.

The regulations implemented in Title IX were binary (based on two genders—male and female), recognizing biological distinctions where they matter and prohibiting discrimination based on biological sex (gender), as Congress intended until now.

On July 12, 2022, the United States Department of Education (USDOE) published in the Federal Register a Notice of Proposed Rulemaking to rewrite the federal regulations governing Title IX.

The proposed revised regulations would expand the scope of Title IX, without Congressional approval, to include prohibiting "discrimination on the basis of sexual orientation and gender identity."

This effective rewrite of Title IX's fundamental purpose has many devastating consequences for parental rights, Free Speech, Free Exercise of Religion, girls' sports, and children's health and safety.

Here's what the new regulations do:

Create a New Category of Sex Discrimination Based on Sexual Orientation and Gender Identity

They declare that preventing a student from participating in any school activity "consistent with their gender identity" subjects that student to harm.

The foolishness of this thinking is obvious. What about the harm to the girls who do not want biological males in their showers and restrooms? Failure to follow the new rules will risk loss of federal funding.

The amendments to Title IX make upholding biological reality a form of "Sex-based Harassment."

In place of "sexual harassment," the new language is "sex-based harassment." Actions like using a child's given name and biologically accurate pronouns instead of a preferred name and pronouns may be regarded as sex-based harassment.

What about parental rights?

The new regulations require K-12 schools to affirm a child's asserted gender identity as a matter of federal law and will involve school officials in life-altering decisions affecting the health and well-being of children. They will further encourage school officials to usurp parental authority without notice to or the consent of, and even over the objections of parents when it comes to gender identity. This will potentially drive a wedge between children and their parents at the time when children need parents most.

The regulations also expand Title IX's reach to include what occurs outside of school. Because they deem failure to treat students consistent with their gender identity subjects that student to harm, activists will be able to report to state child protective services parents who uphold biological reality and refuse to allow school officials to endorse their child's discordant gender identity.

Since this would be federal law, the obligation to comply with the proposed regulations is not "alleviated by any state or local law or other requirement." Therefore, these regulations will create legal uncertainty about the enforceability of state laws protecting parental rights where they conflict with the new federal Title IX regulations. Any such regulation will be exploited by activist officials and likely require expensive court action to obtain a resolution to the conflicts.

WOKE ideology requires schools to open restrooms and lockers based on gender identity.

Schools are required to permit biological males who identify as females to use private facilities set aside for females and vice versa. Girls/women will have to surrender their right to privacy and be placed at increased risk for harassment or assault by males who claim female identity. Reports of how such foolishness has already led to rapes abound.

WOKE ideology threatens to jeopardize female athletic and educational opportunities.

These rules require sex-separate sports to be based on gender identity instead of biological gender, thereby forcing girls and women to compete on an unfair basis for athletic opportunities and scholarships against males and creating significant risks of injury for them.

WOKE proponents want to promote and normalize gender identity ideology in schools as mandated policy and wrongfully encourage students to believe "children can be born into the wrong body."

The harm of such error is never mentioned by the left. They do not mention the emotional, spiritual, physical, and social harm caused by experimenting with gender transitioning.

None of these potential harms were contemplated by Congress when they enacted Title IX in 1972. Parents, faith and community leaders, and educators must speak out courageously and clearly about the many destructive consequences these regulations have.

It took fifty years to reverse Roe v. Wade and the right of unborn babies to be born is still threated at the state and national level by politicians hellbent on assuring a right to "safe and legal abortion services." Abortion has never been safe for an unborn child!

I love God the Father, God the Son, and God the Holy Spirit. My wife and I so love and respect the Bible we read through the Old Testament yearly, and the New Testament twice each year. We believe, with all our hearts, what the Bible says. Children are born the gender God intends for them. From the beginning God intends for marriage to be a covenant between one man and woman to love and cherish each other until death they do part.

It is time for people to stand up, suit up, vote according to Bible Standard, and pray!

The website article http://childparentrights.org/title-IX/ http://childparentrights.org/title-IX/ is extremely informative. I recommend it and recommend listening to Dutch Sheet's Daily Give Him 15 app, available by email or cellphone.

Let me end this chapter with a short decree.

I decree the plots of the devil through the liberal politicians, WOKE, critical race theory, etc. will be understood, resisted, and overturned. Let the crimes against babies in (and outside) the womb; the disgrace of same gender marriage and the like be exposed and understood as sin which has the power to destroy the country we love.

Chapter Seven

Power to Complete Our Mission

The called-out ones did their part in fulfilling the Great Commission. The Book of Acts and the Epistles share how they were witnesses for Christ in Jerusalem, in all Judea, and Samaria, and to the ends of the earth.

When the righteous comprehend and yield to Jesus' commission, they become salt and light to the world. They begin to think like God thinks and do what Jesus did, and when they do so, they brighten their corners of their cities, states, and nations. Let's look at it.

A power promise accompanies the Great Commission in each Gospel and Acts.

The Ekklesia must grasp what Jesus empowered her to do in each of the four Gospels and the Book of Acts. In this chapter we will take a brief look at the specific power promise given alongside the commission released by Jesus in each of the four Gospels: Matthew, Mark, Luke, John, and the Book of Acts.

Commission and Power Promise from Matthew: Authority and Assignment.

📕 Then Jesus came to them and said, *"All authority* in heaven and on earth has been given to me. *Therefore go* **and make disciples of all nations,** baptizing them in the name of the Father and of the Son and of the Holy Spirit, and teaching them to obey everything I have commanded you. **And surely I am with you always,** to the very end of the age." Matthew 28:18–20 NIV. <small>Emphasis mine.</small>

Here Jesus matched His assignment with His authority (the right to act on His behalf) and promise of His continuing presence.

Commission and Power Promise from Mark: Signs and Protection.

📕 He said to them, "Go into all the world and preach the good news to all creation. Whoever believes and is baptized will be saved, but whoever does not believe will be condemned. And **these signs will accompany those who believe:** In my name they will drive out demons; they will speak in new tongues; they will pick up snakes with their hands; and when they drink deadly poison, **it will not hurt them at all**; they will place their hands on sick people, and they will get well."
Mark 16:15–18 NIV. <small>Emphasis mine.</small>

How I wish I had received the truth in the above verses in those powerless years when I tried to minister apart from what Jesus promised in the Gospels and Acts.

Power Promise from Luke: Power and Promise.

📖 You are witnesses of these things. I am going to send you what my Father has promised; but stay in the city **until you have been clothed with power from on high.** Luke 24:48-49 NIV. Emphasis mine.

I entered ministry long before I was clothed with power from on high. I had power to witness but lacked the power that witnesses. I prayed for the sick but seldom saw anyone healed. I prayed for miracles but never witnessed them until I was clothed with power from on high.

Power Promise from John:
Peace, Spirit Filling, and Authority.

It took me years to understand this power promise. I took my first church in the summer of 1976 and entered my calling to pastor and preach. I did my best in my own strength, and every church I pastored grew numerically, at least for a season.

Then I began ministering deliverance and deep healing to people with greater needs than I had tried dealing with previously. I memorized John chapters fourteen and fifteen and began crying out to do the things Jesus did (John 14:12) and be a friend of Jesus, so I could learn everything Jesus learned from the Father (John 15:15). For me, that was key to learning how to do what Abba Father is doing and speak what He is speaking.

I was so hungry to be used by God like the early disciples were, I went on a forty-day food fast. I was quite disappointed during most of the fast. I lost forty pounds but did not experience the heart and life shaping revelation I was looking for until near the end of my fast when an advertisement from Charisma magazine jumped off the page to me. It was for the Wagner Leadership Institute.

I was already leading seminars on deliverance in local churches. The Lord began breaking my religious paradigms and calling me into the greater works of Jesus.

At one seminar I sensed God telling me to blow on a woman coming up for prayer. I resisted the thought. I had last brushed my teeth 12 hours before. Since then, I enjoyed breakfast, lunch, and dinner. I argued with the Lord, "my breath is terrible." He was insistent, so I blew on her and she fell to the floor in what I later learned was "being slain in the Spirit." I thought it might be my bad breath and determined not to do that again. The next person came up and I laid my hands on him and he fell to the floor. I thought, "guess I won't do that either." The next person came forward and all I did was raise my hands without touching the person. If I remember correctly, the person right in front of me and some behind them fell in the Spirit. I had no idea what God was doing to them. I did not understand what He was doing to me. I did realize He was doing something tangible in me.

The following morning, I asked God about blowing on people, and He led me to study the commission and power promise from Luke.

📖 Then said Jesus to them again, Peace [be] unto you: as [my] Father hath sent me, even so send I you. And when he had said this, **he breathed on [them], and saith unto them, receive ye the Holy Ghost: Whosesoever sins ye remit, they are remitted unto them;** [and] whose soever [sins] ye retain, they are retained. John 20:21–23 KJV. <small>Emphasis mine.</small>

God first directed me to study the Greek word translated "breathed" on them. The Greek implies "blowing a puff of air," just like I was led to do when the first person went down in the power of the Holy Spirit. My editor was compelled to say: Yes, but this is life-giving God-anointed TRANSFORMATIONAL Holy Spirit breathing… not just blowing air on a person. It's ELOHIM creational breathing like in Genesis.

Later he led me to study the word translated "remit" in the King James Version. It is often translated "forgive." The correct translation of "remit," used in the King James Version, Darby, and others, is far more powerful.

📖 **Whosesoever sins ye remit, they are remitted unto them;** [and] whose soever [sins] ye retain, they are retained. John 20:23 Darby. <small>Emphasis mine.</small>

Jesus wants us to remit (cancel or refrain from exacting or inflicting a debt or punishment) sins when they are confessed. It is amazing to what the release of freedom from shame and guilt when we simply follow Jesus' instructions by telling a person after their confession, "Your sin is remitted in Jesus' Name." We have found this remission of sin extremely helpful when someone confesses and repents of committing adultery or having an abortion.

John 20:23 not only releases authority to us to remit sins, but it also encourages us to do so!

Power Promise from Acts:
Holy Spirit Baptism to get the job done.

📖 And He said to them, "It is not for you to know times or seasons which the Father has put in His own authority. ⁸ But you shall receive power when the Holy Spirit has come upon you; and you shall be witnesses to Me in Jerusalem, and in all Judea and Samaria, and to the end of the earth."
Acts 1:7–8.

Before Pentecost, Peter was a well-meaning and zealous follower of Jesus. He was a teeter-totter follower, sometimes way up and sometimes all the way down. He was usually the first to recognize what God was up to in and through Jesus. It was Peter who jumped out of boat in faith, but then began to sink in fear. He said he would never deny Jesus but denied Him three times before the rooster crowed twice.

Something got into Peter, however. Cowardly and hot then cold Peter became a mighty apostle and preacher when he received Holy Spirit filling.

Like Peter, we have a job to do that is far too big to do in soulish weakness. We need men and women like Peter who receive the fullness of Holy Spirit as they fully surrender themselves to God.

God was willing to spare Sodom and Gomorrah if only ten righteous people could be found. Abraham prayed for grace if ten could be found. I can see him counting off his fingers thinking of his relatives in Sodom: Lot, Lot's wife, his two married daughters and their husband, plus his two unmarried daughters and their fiancée's, ten in all. Unfortunately, though they numbered ten, they were not all righteous. Therefore, Sodom and Gomorrah were destroyed by fire.

How many righteous people are in government?

I wonder how many righteous people can be found in every nation's and state's capitals. How many righteous people can be found in our city, state, and national government? I contend that no one who legislates contrary to the Word of God in matters like the right for babies to live, traditional marriage, gender transitioning, etc. is righteous.

2 Chronicles chapter twenty tells of a time when Israel was backed up against the wall with pagan armies about to invade and destroy the land. The entire chapter is fascinating, but I will just share a key statement made by Jehoshaphat, King of Judah.

📖 Jehoshaphat stood and said, "Hear me, O Judah and you inhabitants of Jerusalem: Believe in the Lord your God, and you **shall be established**; believe His prophets, and **you shall prosper**." 2 Chronicles 20:20b. Emphasis mine.

A rudimentary faith in the existence of God is enough to establish and keep us. We must hear and act upon what God is saying through His prophets if we want help individuals and governments to prosper. We need to grasp the hem of Jesus' garment for our communities, but that is not enough. We need to take His yoke and follow Jesus to bring transformation to the cities, state, and nations we live in.

We can't do it without God ~
God won't do it without us.

Chapter Eight

What I hear God saying for 5783 and beyond

I was asked to give an eight-minute talk at a Breakthrough Apostolic Ministry Network meeting concerning what I heard the Lord speaking as the head of the Hebrew year 5783. I think it is fitting here.

If I were to address what I sense God saying for our home state of Michigan, I would highlight the need to address marine spirits because Michigan is nearly surrounded by water and the rule of marine spirits over many of our port cities as is evident by crime, poverty, iniquity, and disrespect for life, etc. If I were to address what I sense God saying about my city, I would say we need to address the failure of churches to win the lost and bring them all the way into the Kingdom of Heaven. If I were to address what God is saying to our local Church, I would address prayerlessness. We do need to intentionally address these things. Above all this, however, God is loudly speaking to me about:

Be Careful little mouths what you speak.

At the Head of the Year, 5783 the Lord again convicted me of the power of words. Even though I am right about the way the left, WOKE, and godless agendas are perpetuated by enemies of the Kingdom of God, I am wrong when I allow hatred to spew forth through cursing.

All human cursing empowers the enemy's agenda.

📖 Thou shalt decree a thing and it shall be established unto you. Job 22:28.

If we declare good things like, "The Lord is my Healer," we will walk in better health. If we decree bad things like, "It is going to be a bad flu season, I better stock up on flu medicines and/or get vaccinated," we are more likely to get sick. Decreeing health has worked very well for me. Even though I used to have stomach flu at least once a year, I have not even had flu symptoms more than once in the past twenty-five years or more, and that was after a Free Mason release.

Could it be that those who stand against truth, righteousness, and a biblical worldview gain traction through the power of our cursing them? I see how that might open the door for the enemy to kill, steal, and destroy them—and us!

I confess I have cursed certain politicians who have been used to empower Baal, Molech, Antichrist and other principalities, powers, and authorities.

On June 26, 2015, when the Supreme Court legalized same-sex marriage in every state and Obama displayed gay pride colors on the White House, I prayed he would have a Nebuchadnezzar moment. My prayer was not answered. Perhaps that prayer has been answered, in part, for President Joe Biden, but God is convicting me not to follow the example of the left's political campaigns of defaming their opponent's character by twisting everything good they have done into something bad, as we see in far too many political campaigns. God calls us to bless, not curse.

My imprecatory prayers from Psalm109:6–9 have not been answered either. The Antichrist, woke, and leftist politicians have not yet been judged and found guilty. They may be soon, but Holy Spirit tells me I am supposed to bless my enemies rather than curse them. Others have not yet taken their offices. Their children and spouses have not been bereaved. Perhaps that is because my heart has not been right concerning our political enemies. As Jesus said,

📖 43 "You have heard that it was said, 'You shall love your neighbor and hate your enemy.' 44 But I say to you, love your enemies, bless those who curse you, do good to those who hate you, and pray for those who spitefully use you and persecute you, 45 that you may be sons of your Father in heaven; (WOW) for He makes His sun rise on the evil and on the

good, and sends rain on the just and on the unjust.
Bless and do not curse.
Matthew 5:43–45. Emphasis mine.

We need to stand against evil ideologies but not curse
individuals. We should stand, and we to fight—but
with right hearts!

📖 Death and life are in the power of the tongue, and
those who love it will eat its fruit. Proverbs 18:21.

Could it be we are eating the fruit of godless politicians
because we have cursed, rather than blessed them with
our prayers and decrees? We must guard our hearts in
this new year. Every mouth problem begins with a
heart problem.

📖 Jesus said, But those things which proceed out of
the mouth come from the heart, and they defile a
man. Matthew 15:18.

📖 A good man out of the good treasure of his heart
brings forth good; and an evil man out of the evil
treasure of his heart brings forth evil. **For out of the
abundance of the heart his mouth speaks**.
Luke 6:45. Emphasis mine.

We must guard our hearts, lest our words defile us!
James wrote,

📖 See how great a forest a little fire kindles! ⁶ And the
tongue is a fire, a world of iniquity. The tongue is

so set among our members that it defiles the whole body and sets on fire the course of nature; and it is set on fire by hell. [8] But no man can tame the tongue. It is an unruly evil, full of deadly poison. [9] With it we bless our God and Father, and with it we curse men, who have been made in the similitude of God. [10] Out of the same mouth proceed blessing and cursing. My brethren, these things ought not to be so. James 3:1–10.

Thankfully, God will tame our tongues IF we ask Him to.

One of my new books this year is Breaking Patterns of Perversity – Freedom from iniquity. Only 8 of the 42 translations I study, rightly translate the Hebrew "avon" as iniquity. The same is true of the wrong translation of the Greek "par-ap'-to-mah" in James 5:16, where only 8 translations properly translate it as faults.

Sins are something we do. Iniquities and faults are done to us and our families by wrongdoings of by our ancestors, governments, and culture passed down to us.

Recently I shared a Tale of Two Women who met the Master (John 4:5–42; 8:1–11). Both women were both bound by sin and judged by everyone, especially the most religious. Jesus met them with unconditional love, acceptance, and forgiveness.

Their lives were changed when Jesus did not join those who condemned them. Instead, He offered grace and mercy and translated them from the kingdom of darkness to the kingdom of light. We must go and do likewise!

Jesus wants us to bless and not curse. And that is exactly what we will do if we seek first the Kingdom of God and His righteousness. So help me God, so help us!

It is time to speak up, pray up, and pay up.

We need to suit up and step up to steer America back to its covenant roots. At the same time, God wants us to be winsome.

We must study the issues and support godly politicians and causes. We must read between the lines, especially every time we prepare to vote. We should never vote for anyone who is pro-abortion, even if they are a friend or relative. Abortion is never safe or legal for the unborn.

I wrote the following Letter to the Editor which was published on October 15, 2022.

> Governor Whitmer, with unusual honesty and candor says, "I will fight like hell to keep abortion safe and legal in Michigan." She does fight like hell (and I think, in partnership with hell) concerning abortion. Her attorney general,

Dana Nessel, refuses to enforce the law concerning abortion. She heinously fights to protect the so-called right of a mother to have an abortion at any time for any reason. I was taught Legislators pass laws. The law-making factory in Lansing has created a plethora of them. An attorney's duty, however, is to enforce the law, not pick and choose which laws they will put into effect.

Abortion is never safe for an unborn child! Unborn children are people, not fetuses! Through consistent Bible study we understand every child is chosen and appointed to do certain things for God even before being formed in the womb. (Jeremiah 1:7) We read how every person is God's workmanship, created in Christ Jesus with specific destiny to fulfill during their lives to bless the world. (Ephesians 2:10) We read how intricately God is involved as each child is formed within his or her mother's womb. (Psalm 139:13–17)

Abortion not only kills children, but it also cancels their God-given destiny to bless society.

One reason our country suffers such lack of qualified workers and politicians is because every abortion snuffs out a destiny designed to bring blessing to every area of society. Abortion is not birth control! Abortion kills babies and their destinies. Vote prolife.

We need to speak up and pray up!

Jesus seldom expressed anger but three of the Gospels quote Him saying "My house shall me called a house a prayer."

📖 And He said to them, "It is written, 'My house shall be called house of prayer,' but you have made it a 'den of thieves.'" Matthew 21:23.

Matthew shares how Jesus overturned the tables of the money changers and the seats of those who sold doves. We have focused on what they were doing wrong.

We have missed what God's people **were not doing** right. We are to be a house of prayer! There was a time when my wife, Pamela, led a 9:00 p.m. to midnight time of prayer every Thursday night. Few came. There was a time when we did a weekday morning prayer. Few came. For years I've tried to get people to meet at 9:30 a.m. on Sundays to pray before service starts. Few came. Now so we meet for 10 minutes at 9:40 a.m. Sadly, only a few meet and fewer still lead out in prayer.

I am grateful more people are sharing and praying as God leads them on Sunday mornings. I love to pray and decree during worship—though I will love it even more when others do so. It is time to realize it will take God's people crying out to God to save our country.

📖 And My people on whom My name is called be humbled, and pray, and seek My face, and turn back from their evil ways, then I -- I hear from the heavens, and forgive their sin, and heal their land. 2 Chronicles 7:14 TLV.

📖 And My people (who are known by My name) humbly pray, follow My commandments, and abandon any actions or thoughts that might lead to further sinning, then I shall hear *their prayers* from *My house in* heaven. 2 Chronicles 7:14 Voice. 2 Chronicles 7:14 VOICE.

📖 God appeared to Solomon that very night and said, "I accept your prayer; yes, I have chosen this place as a temple for sacrifice, a house of worship. If I ever shut off the supply of rain from the skies or order the locusts to eat the crops or send a plague on my people, and my people, my God-defined people, respond by humbling themselves, praying, seeking my presence, and turning their backs on their wicked lives, I'll be there ready for you: I'll listen from heaven, forgive their sins, and restore their land to health. From now on I'm alert day and night to the prayers offered at this place. 2 Chronicles 7:14 MSG.

Chapter Nine

The Greatest of These . . . in a WOKE Culture

While driving to a nursing home, I noticed a large rainbow sign that caught my attention. It says, "Love Trumps Hate."

I assume it encourages others to love and accept people regardless of their gender preference or attraction to people of the same or different gender. We ARE to love and accept others. Amen? But if it promotes gender fluidity, I am surprised it had "Trump" in the center of the sign. Donald Trump, unlike Joe Biden, stands for traditional marriage and protecting babies from abortion.

I doubt Donald Trump agreed with the liberal crowd, or the Disney Empire which sued Florida's governor for insisting parents have the right to protect their Kindergarten through third grade children from being taught about choosing whatever gender they desire according to their current emotional leaning, peer pressure, or hidden agenda of WOKE teachers.

There are people fighting to teach four-to-ten-year old's they can choose to be whatever gender they want to be, even to the point of prescribing sex changing drugs at a young age.

What is WOKE?

- Oxford dictionaries: Adjective 1. alert to injustice and discrimination in society, especially racism: informal "we need to stay angry and stay woke" OK? but Christians have always been on the front line of social justice.

- Woke meaning 2. What does 'woke' actually mean? A person who is woke is typically considered to be sensitive to and aware of racial or social discrimination or injustice that they themselves are not experiencing, but that doesn't have to be the case. The definition for 'woke' was added to the Oxford English Dictionary in 2017.

Some of the goals of the woke culture are to dissolve the nuclear family, abolish capitalism, eliminate religion, rewrite the U.S. Constitution, and raise children gender neutral. NOT OK. Such goals are in direct opposition to the Bible and to Bible believing people. The fight is heating up! It is not going to get easier until we go to heaven!

**We are in a time when we must commit
to come back to the Bible and live it.**

📖 [13] But he who endures to the end shall be saved. Matthew 24:13. Emphasis mine.

We are in a season to lovingly challenge people with truth.

📖 [9] Do you not know that the unrighteous will not inherit the kingdom of God? Do not be deceived. Neither fornicators, nor idolaters, nor adulterers, nor homosexuals, nor sodomites, [10] nor thieves, nor covetous, nor drunkards, nor revilers, nor extortioners will inherit the kingdom of God. 1 Corinthians 6:9–10.

Is it loving to not reach people living in damning delusion? Hell is a real place!

We must love and accept people before we can expect them to listen to the Gospel. We must learn to love sinners the way Jesus loved the Samaritan woman at the well and the woman who was caught in the very act of adultery. We need to love leftist businesspeople as Jesus loved the despised tax-collector Zacchaeus. Our love is their only chance!

We are in a season to do our best to make sure people are truly saved.

When Jesus becomes an invited guest in a person's life, He starts cleaning them up! It is impossible to have both the pure Son of God living within and sin reigning in a life!

📖 Therefore, if anyone is in Christ, he is a new creation; old things have passed away; behold, all things have become new. 2 Corinthians 5:17.

1 Corinthians 6:9–19 says the unrighteous will not inherit the Kingdom of God. Paul named several things that prevent entrance to the Kingdom: fornication, idolatry, adultery, same gender sex, theft, covetousness, drunkenness, reviling and extortion. They give the truth according to God and the Bible. Galatians 5:19–21 gives a similar list:

📖 [19] Now the works of the flesh are evident, which are: adultery, fornication, uncleanness, lewd-ness, [20]idolatry, sorcery, hatred, contentions, jealousies, outbursts of wrath, selfish ambitions, dissensions, heresies, [21] envy, murders, drunkenness, revelries, and the like; of which I tell you beforehand, just as I also told you in time past, that those who practice such things will not inherit the kingdom of God. Galatians 5:19–21.

God does not give such lists so we can use them as clubs to beat people up. We should operate from the Tree of Life — not the tree of the knowledge of good and evil. (Explained in the Addendum of my book *From Woe is Me to Wow is He!)*

Lists like those in Galatians five and 1 Corinthians 6 would be seem hopeless, had Jesus not paid such a price to redeem us! He makes it possible to exchange old lives for new ones—and help others to do the same. I am thrilled God inspired Paul to add verse 11 to 1 Corinthians 6:9–10.

📖 And **such were some of you**. But you were washed, but you were sanctified, but you were justified in the name of the Lord Jesus and by the Spirit of our God. 1 Corinthians 6:11. Emphasis mine.

> **When people are really saved,**
> **they are saved FROM their old life**
> **TO brand-new lives, guided by Holy Spirit**
> **who takes up residence in them.**

Jesus' great Commission is making disciples of all nations—teaching them to live in the freedom Jesus paid for with His own blood. He tells us to heal the sick, cast out demons, and advance the Kingdom of God.

I was thinking on these things while prayer walking. It was a beautiful day; the sun was rising enough I was able to make out twenty or more deer in four different spots. I was pondering some notes I glanced at in the NKJV Open Bibles Pam, and I are using this year. I thought of the verse where Paul says, "The Greatest of these is love."

Paul discerns spiritual giftedness by the kind of love God demonstrated by sending His only begotten Son, and the love Jesus demonstrated by laying down His life for sinners. We love Him because He first loved us. Paul says our giftedness has little value unless it flows from hearts that love God and people, including Pre-Christian sinners. He then concludes,

📖 And now abide faith, hope, love, these three; but the greatest of these is love. 1 Corinthians 13:13.

**Genuine love is what gives genuine
Believers a voice in WOKE Culture.**

We should not expect people to listen to us unless we treat them with love, honor, and respect. Witness starts with "WITHNESS." If we think we are too good to associate with sinners, they will not give a rip about how much we know about the Bible.

**People won't care how much we know
until they know how much we care!**

Let me share some things I modified from the footnotes of our Open Bibles. They show characteristics that make Believers winsome in today's culture regardless of cultural norms, or what the Bible would call abnormal!

First is, a Changed Life. The first stanza of a famous Christian Song begins: "what a wonderful change in my life has been wrought since Jesus came into my heart."

Without a doubt the greatest proof of the new birth is a changed life.

When one truly becomes a child of God, they suddenly love the following:

A mark of true Children of God is we love Jesus.

Before conversion sinners might hold Christ in high esteem, but after conversion they love the Savior.

📖 Whoever believes that Jesus is the Christ is born of God, and everyone who loves Him who begot also loves him who is begotten of Him. ² By this we know that we love the children of God, when we love God and keep His commandments.
1 John 5:1–2.

A mark of true Children of God is we love the Bible.

We should love God's Word as the psalmist did in Psalm 119 where he expresses his great love for God's Word no less than seventeen times. See verses from Psalm 119:

📖 Your testimonies also are my delight and my counselors. V. 24.

📖 Behold, I long for Your precepts; Revive me in Your righteousness. V. 40.

📖 And I will delight myself in Your commandments, Which I love.⁴⁸ My hands also I will lift up to Your commandments, Which I love, And I will meditate on Your statutes. Vs. 47–48.

📖 The law of Your mouth is better to me than thousands of coins of gold and silver. V. 72.

📖 Oh, how I love Your law! It is my meditation all the day. V. 97.

📖 How sweet are Your words to my taste, Sweeter than honey to my mouth! V. 103.

📖 Your testimonies I have taken as a heritage forever, for they are the rejoicing of my heart. V. 111.

📖 I hate the double-minded, but I love Your law. V. 113.

📖 It is time for You to act, O Lord, for they have regarded Your law as void. Therefore I love Your commandments More than gold, yes, than fine gold! Vs. 126–127.

📖 Your testimonies are wonderful; therefore my soul keeps them. V. 129.

📖 Your word is very pure; therefore Your servant loves it. V. 140.

📖 Trouble and anguish have overtaken me, Yet Your commandments are my delights. V. 143.

📖 Consider how I love Your precepts; Revive me, O Lord, according to Your lovingkindness. V. 159.

📖 I rejoice at Your word as one who finds great treasure. V. 162.

📖 Great peace have those who love Your law, And nothing causes them to stumble. V. 165.

📖 I keep Your precepts and Your testimonies, for all my ways are before You. V. 168.

Believers love God's Word, but that is not all.

A mark of true Children of God is loving other Believers.

Years ago, I attended Spartan Store Conventions, where I felt out of place because of my low position as a grocery clerk. When I became a pastor, I felt "less-than" when I attended meetings with pastors who had churches much larger than mine.

I laugh at the story of a man being escorted through heaven by an angel. They came to a place with high walls and the angel said, "be quiet, —this is the ultra-fundamentalist section, and they think they are the only ones here."

We are to love all Believers, not just those of our personal persuasion.

📖 We know that we have passed from death to life, because we love the brethren. He who does not love his brother abides in death.1 John 3:14.

When I pondered this, I thought of a song from back when I was first saved. Perhaps you remember it too, "They will know we are Christians by our love."

A mark of true Children of God is we love our enemies.

It is easy to love people who think like we think. But, to change our world we must start loving people who think opposite the way we do. Including WOKE people.

📖 43 "You have heard that it was said, 'You shall love your neighbor and hate your enemy.' 44 But I say to you, love your enemies, bless those who curse you, do good to those who hate you, and pray for those who spitefully use you and persecute you, 45 that you may be sons of your Father in heaven; for He makes His sun rise on the evil and on the good, and sends rain on the just and on the unjust.
Matthew 5:43–45.

A mark of true Children of God is we love the souls of all people.

If we truly love PEOPLE, we will be concerned for their souls. Do we love the lost enough to cry out for their conversion?

📖 Brethren, my heart's desire and prayer to God for Israel is that they may be saved. Romans 10:1.

📖 For the love of Christ compels us, because we judge thus: that if One died for all, then all died; 2 Corinthians 5:14.

A mark of true Children of God is we love the pure life.

📖 [15] Do not love the world or the things in the world. If anyone loves the world, the love of the Father is not in him. [16] For all that is in the world—the lust of the flesh, the lust of the eyes, and the pride of life—is not of the Father but is of the world. [17] And the world is passing away, and the lust of it; but he who does the will of God abides forever. 1 John 2:15–17.

📖 For whatever is born of God overcomes the world. And this is the victory that has overcome the world—our faith. 1 John 5:4.

A mark of true Children of God is we love to share our hearts and spirits with God and one another.

📖 speaking to one another in psalms and hymns and spiritual songs, singing and making melody in your heart to the Lord. Ephesians 5:19.

Jesus summed up the Law and the Prophets With: Love for God and others.

Most people have no idea what true love is. They understand lust and rallying around ideas like WOKE. Black Lives Matter, Critical Race Theory, Defund the

Police, and either sides of things like abortion or pro-live, traditional, or same gender marriage.

They argue about accepting one's gender or promoting treatment to change gender. People rally around political parties and people. Even people who cannot define "woman" desire love and acceptance.

**Deep down, everyone wants
to be loved and accepted.**

**Loving the unlovable is hard for religious people —
not so much for Spirit filled people.**

📖 34But when the Pharisees heard that He had silenced the Sadducees, they gathered together. 35Then one of them, a lawyer, asked Him a question, testing Him, and saying, 36 "Teacher, which is the great commandment in the law?"

Love has greater power than theological greatness!

📖 37 Jesus said to him, "'You shall love the Lord your God with all your heart, with all your soul, and with all your mind.' 38 This is the first and great commandment. 39 And the second is like it: 'You shall love your neighbor as yourself.' 40 On these two commandments hang all the Law and the Prophets." Matthew 22: 34–40.

You would think an understanding of the first and second greatest commandment would be enough. But people fail to get. So, liberals and conservatives throw sticks and stones at one another. Liberals defund the police, crowd, loot and destroy the properties of those who want to provide services to their communities and make an honest living. They don't even seem to realize they are hating and destroying their neighbors and neighborhoods. But conservatives can be plain mean, nasty, and judgmental too. Such ought not to be!

Jesus made it clear who our neighbor really is.

📖 25 And behold, a certain lawyer stood up and tested Him, saying, "Teacher, what shall I do to inherit eternal life?" 26 He said to him, "What is written in the law? What is your reading of it?" Matthew 10:25–26.

📖 27 So he answered and said, "'You shall love the Lord your God with all your heart, with all your soul, with all your strength, and with all your mind,' and 'your neighbor as yourself.'" 28 And He said to him, "You have answered rightly; do this and you will live." Matthew 10:27–28.

The man asked a question we must consider: "Who is my neighbor?"

📖 29 But he, wanting to justify himself, said to Jesus, "And who is my neighbor?" Matthew 10:29.

Before we continue: Do you really want to know how your neighbor is doing? Do you really want to know whom God holds YOU responsible for?

📖 30 Then Jesus answered and said: "A certain man went down from Jerusalem to Jericho, and fell among thieves, who stripped him of his clothing, wounded him, and departed, leaving him half dead. 31 Now by chance a certain priest came down that road. And when he saw him, he passed by on the other side. 32 Likewise a Levite, when he arrived at the place, came and looked, and passed by on the other side. Matthew 10:30–32.

How many people do we pass by on the other side?

📖 33 But a certain Samaritan, as he journeyed, came where he was. And when he saw him, he had compassion. 34 So he went to him and bandaged his wounds, pouring on oil and wine; and he set him on his own animal, brought him to an inn, and took care of him.

📖 35 On the next day, when he departed, he took out two denarii, gave them to the innkeeper, and said to him, 'Take care of him; and whatever more you spend, when I come again, I will repay you.' Matthew 10:33–35.

We love the parable of the Good Samaritan more than we like the idea of being Good Samaritans.

I confess I struggle with loving people when biblical standards are scoffed, ignored, or twisted to support twisted views of marriage, parenting, social justice, education, life of the unborn, public decency, promotion of cannabis businesses built on greed and covetousness. There are some things we must stand for and other things we need to stand against. Jesus stood so clearly, He submitted to crucifixion. Still, He kept His love on, even telling the repentant thief on the cross—you know, the one who mocked Him earlier, "Today you will be with me in Paradise."

Jesus never stopped being a friend of sinners—neither should we!

He ate with sinners and drunkards. He let a woman of poor reputation wash His feet with His hair. He was a good neighbor to bad neighbors.

Jesus lovingly, but firmly confronted Saul of Tarsus who was on mission to drag Believers to prison, and his life was changed. He reinstated Peter who denied Him three times. He accepted an immoral woman at a well, talked with her, and she was transformed into the town's evangelist. He looked at a man who was born blind and scorned because people though he or his parents sinned, but Jesus healed him.

Jesus accepted people where they were and from there, led them into truth.

The best way to change our world is one person at a time—like Jesus did. The only hope for the WOKE crowd, the only hope for those confused by Critical Race Theory, the only hope for the addict, drug pusher, and drunkard is for God's People to love the Lord their God with all their heart, soul, mind, and strength, so they might love their neighbor as they love themselves. I leave you today with what Jesus said to the man who wondered what the greatest and second greatest commandments were.

📖 [36] So which of these three do you think was neighbor to him who fell among the thieves?" [37] And he said, "He who showed mercy on him." Then Jesus said to him, "Go and do likewise." Matthew 10:36–37.

Chapter Ten

It is Time to Identify the Real Enemy.

I debated whether to include this chapter because many people do not have a well-defined concept of spiritual warfare. Even though the Bible tells us "We do not wrestle against flesh and blood" (Ephesians 6:12), many strong conservatives have very limited understanding of the spiritual enemies we face.

In May 2022, my home state, Michigan, twelve cities were overrun with protesters carrying proabortion signs. National news network showed videos of similar protests throughout the county.

Our world has gone crazy. Riots, WOKE, Critical Race Theory, Inflation, escalating prices for food (when it is available). The price of gas, utilities, housing, and living has never been higher in America. Scandals abound, as does homelessness, abuse, divorce, gun violence, addiction and on and on. There is something bigger at work than China, Russia, progressiveness, the WOKE crowd, Critical Race Theorists, Leftists, progressives, and liberals. It is bigger than people who have become reprobate because they do not want to retain in themselves the knowledge of God (Romans 1:28–32).

So, who is the real enemy? Are there things more sinister than antichrist values working behind the scenes, hellbent on destroying the Judeo-Christian ethic that makes families, states, and nations great? Perhaps it is time to get back to the Bible. We will start with a verse you can probably quote.

📖 For we do not wrestle against flesh and blood, but against principalities, against powers, against the rulers of the darkness of this age, against spiritual *hosts* of wickedness in the heavenly *places.* Ephesians 6:10.

The problem is not the foes we face ~ the real problem is that we wrestle not!

For fifty years the church has by and large retreated within the four walls of their brick-and-mortar buildings. When I answered the call to preach, the first thing my father tried to talk me into was taking over his excavating business. There would have been a lot more money in that, but money isn't everything. Had I known then what I know now, I would have told him spiritual warfare is spiritual excavating—uncovering God's redemptive purpose for a place and digging down to find where the foundations need repair.

Dad did support my call to preach after I turned down his offer to buy his business. But he warned me to stay away from politics and money. Unfortunately, the Church has done that and has reaped what it has sown: Government and society without Christian influence. Are you OK with the way things are in our state and country? All that is necessary for the triumph of good over evil is for God's people to do nothing.

If we do not become more vigilant, we will lose the war for our families, and for America by default.

We have distanced ourselves too far from the "Give me liberty or give me death" commitment that made America the strongest nation on earth. So let me pose the question Cindy Williams Moore threw at the leaders who met together in Mt. Pleasant.

Where and what is the battle?
Paul tells us it goes deeper than
environment, economy, and government.

📖 For we are not wrestling with flesh and blood [contending only with physical opponents], but against the despotisms, against the powers, against [the master spirits who are] the world rulers of this present darkness, against the spirit forces of wickedness in the heavenly (supernatural) sphere. Ephesians 6:10 AMPC.

Cindy believes we have a two-year window to fight the battle and restore Michigan to God's redemptive purpose. She asked us to identify the warfronts. We must understand the powers working behind governmental officials who are already politicking to make sure abortion remains accessible in Michigan when Roe v. Wade is overturned.

Who are the real enemies?

We are deceived if we think the real enemy is WOKEISM, Pro-abortion thinking, Critical Race Theory, LGBTQ+-, ETC. Behind our flesh and blood enemies are principalities, powers, rulers of darkness, and spiritual forces of evil in the heavenly realms. There are partnerships and alliances between demonic powers that gain access through humans, who come into agreement with their deception.

Warfront One: The partnership of Baal and Molech.

Baal is mentioned 700 times in the Old Testament and once in Romans. The first mention of Baal is in Genesis.

📖 When Saul died, **Baal**-Hanan the son of Achbor reigned in his place. Genesis 36:38.

I take the following from a Got Questions.org about Baal.

Baal was the name of the supreme god worshiped in ancient Canaan and Phoenicia.

The practice of Baal worship infiltrated Jewish religious life during the time of the Judges (Judges 3:7), became widespread in Israel during the reign of Ahab (1 Kings 16:31–33) and also affected Judah (2 Chronicles 28:1–2). The word baal means "lord"; the plural is baalim. In general, Baal was a fertility god who was believed to enable the earth to produce crops, and people to produce children.

The Canaanites worshiped Baal as the sun god and as the storm god—he is usually depicted holding a lightning bolt—who defeated enemies and produced crops. They also worshiped him as a fertility god who provided children. Baal worship was rooted in sensuality and involved ritualistic prostitution in the temples. At times, appeasing Baal required human sacrifice, usually the firstborn of the one making the sacrifice (Jeremiah 19:5). (Aborting firstborns—cuts family destiny.) The priests of Baal appealed to their god in rites of wild abandon which included loud, ecstatic cries and self-inflicted injury (Cutting) (1 Kings 18:28).

In Matthew 12:27, Jesus calls Satan "Beelzebub," linking the devil to Baal-Zebub, a Philistine deity (2 Kings 1:2). The Baalim of the Old Testament were nothing more than demons masquerading as gods, and all idolatry is ultimately devil-worship (1 Corinthians 10:20). https://www.gotquestions.org/

Molech is only mentioned 8 times. The first mention is in Leviticus.

📖 And you shall not let any of your descendants pass through *the fire* to **Molech**, nor shall you profane the name of your God: I *am* the Lord. Leviticus 18:1.

Here are few more things from GotQuestions.org.

As with many details in ancient history, the exact origin of /Molech worship is unclear. The term Moloch is believed to have originated with the Phoenician mlk, which referred to a type of sacrifice made to confirm or acquit a vow. Melekh is the Hebrew word for "king." It was common for the Israelites to combine the name of pagan gods with the vowels in the Hebrew word for shame: bosheth. This is how the goddess of fertility and war, Astarte, became Ashtoreth. The combination of mlk, melekh, and bosheth results in "Moloch," which could be interpreted as "the personified ruler of shameful sacrifice." It has also been spelled Milcom, Milkim, and Malik. Ashtoreth was his consort, and ritual prostitution was considered an important form of worship.

Moloch worship included child sacrifice, or "passing children through the fire." It is believed that idols of Moloch were giant metal statues of a man with a bull's head. Each image had a hole in the abdomen and possibly outstretched forearms that made a kind of ramp to the hole. A fire was lit in or around the statue. Babies were placed in the statue's arms or in the hole. When a couple sacrificed their firstborn, they believed that Moloch would ensure financial prosperity for the family and future children. Is abortion less barbaric than this?

In Genesis 12 Abraham followed God's call to move to Canaan. Although human sacrifice was not common in Abraham's native Ur, it was well-established in his new land. God later asked Abraham to offer Isaac as a sacrifice (Genesis 22:2).

Baal and Molech partner to offend Jehovah. Their works are seen through works and mindsets that resist God and His Kingdom.

Some indicators of their work include:
➤ Stolen identity, including WOKE,
➤ Orphan mentality,
➤ Stealing children from influence of parents,
➤ Gender Confusion, and
➤ Abortion.

It is horribly taxing on children whose minds and value systems are not well enough developed to handle the suggestion boys can be girls and vice-versa. Too many reports of WOKE and Leftist brain washing in the foundational years of schooling have been reported.

The possibility of a favorable SCOTUS ruling concerning abortion leaked on May 8, 2022, and all hell broke out. I decree it is time for all heaven to break out!

Sacrifice empowers demon gods. Every child sacrificed intentionally or unknowingly to Baal and/or Molech through abortion strengthens the power of the enemy to kill, steal, and destroy. My heart pleads for the healing and deliverance of millions of post-abortive parents. We have ministered to hundreds of post-abortive parents with love, compassion, and grace. Still, the Church of Jesus Christ must bring an end to the legalization and public funding of shedding of innocent blood.

📖 Lest innocent blood be shed in the midst of your land which the Lord your God is giving you *as* an inheritance, **and *thus* guilt of blood-shed be upon you**. Deut. 19:10. Emphasis mine.

📖 So you shall not **pollute the land** where you *are;* for **blood defiles the land**, and no atonement can be made for the land, for the blood that is shed on it, except by the blood of him who shed it.

Numbers 35:33. Emphasis mine.

When you consider all the violent and nonviolent protests concerning overturning Roe v. Wade, you realize defiled our land has become.

Our land is polluted by the shedding of the innocent blood of over 63 million babies in the last 50 years. (The Bible refers to the number 50 as a year of Jubilee!)

Row versus Wade was overturned fifty years after it first passed! Angry politicians across the land promise to fight like hell to keep abortion legal. That is exactly what they are doing—joining hell's fight to ensure demons are empowered by the shedding of innocent blood. Will we join heaven's fight to protect the innocent?

Two things we must do.

1. **We need to tear down the strongholds of Baal and Molech through prayer and spiritual warfare.**

2. **We need to build a biblical worldview.**

Family Research Council has determined less than 6% of those who consider themselves Christian have a Biblical Worldview. We must study the Word of God and the God of the Word to show ourselves and then train others to live and minister according to the Bible.

Warfront 2: The partnership of Python/Sorcery and Mammon.

Python/Sorcery and Mammon partner to offend Jehovah. Their works are seen through works and mindsets that resist God and His Kingdom.

Python and sorcery work through addiction and witchcraft. Mammon is the governmental side, building revenue through businesses that offend God like abortion, Cannabis, Street drugs, Pharmakia, Prostitution, Child trafficking and the like.

Python and sorcery work hand in hand. Python tries to choke the life out of people, especially during deliverance. We often command python to let go of a person's throat or chest before we can expel it. Python occasionally makes people slither like snakes. Sorcery is translated from the Greek word Pharmakia, which we take the English word Pharmacy from. It lures people, as through witchcraft, to addiction to drugs, alcohol, tobacco, vaping and so many other vices. Mammon takes advantage of python's and Pharmakia's works through governmental greed with the promise of great financial gains through rebates to municipalities through taxes and fees places on Cannabis, Alcohol, and the like.

Python/Sorcery and Mammon are in cohorts (partnership) to destroy law and order in every segment of society.

Python and sorcery are the addiction side of this partnership.

Their job is to curse people spiritually through addiction to destroy hope, purpose, and God's prophetic destiny for people He wants to use as Kingdom Movers and Shakers. Addicts often have intellects far above normal before they fall into the bondage of addiction. I read the book *The Devil Loves a Shining Mark* nearly fifty years ago, which was written by a converted mobster in 1971. His story is similar to Mike Lindell, the Pillow Guy, who wrote *Absolute Proof* in 2021.

They were both people of extraordinary destiny, whom the devil tried to destroy through wickedness. The devil is hellbent on destroying called and gifted people. It is time to stand in the gap and break the devil's hold over them.

Mammon is the governmental side of this partnership, luring those in business and government into partnership with destructive evil through the promise of great financial return.

MLive reported on March 28, 2022, Michigan received $172 million in 2021 recreational marijuana tax. Saint Joseph County, Michigan received $169,360 from 3 licenses in 2021 alone. More than $42 million tax dollars from Michigan's recreational marijuana industry were expected to be doled out to 163 counties, villages, and townships in late March or early April. That means each eligible municipality and county will receive more than $56,400 for every licensed retail store and micro business located within its jurisdiction, said the State Treasurer's Office. Some of us fought hard to keep Marijuana businesses from taking over our cities, but we failed to address this scourge with weapons that are not carnal, but spiritual to the taking down of strongholds.

Two more things we need to do.

1. **We need to take down the strongholds of python, sorcery (Pharmakia), and Mammon.**

2. **We need to restore the foundation of Apostles and apostolic (fivefold) gifts, and the Fruit of the Spirit. Galatians 5:22–23.**

A Kingdom understanding of Apostles, Prophets, Evangelists, Pastors, and Teachers is that they are assigned to every segment of society, not just to the church that meets on Sunday mornings. The Kingdom mandate from Genesis to Revelation is for God's people to be fruitful, multiply, and take dominion over the whole earth. The Ekklesia must rise up and do what Jesus calls it to do—advance the Kingdom of God forcibly over the earth (Matthew 11:12).

Are you having fun yet? There is one more warfront to address.

Warfront 3: The partnership of Jezebel and Ahab, including: civil and ecclesiastical government, management and labor, government, citizens, and traditional family.

Jezebel and Ahab partner to offend Jehovah. Their works are seen through efforts and mindsets that resist God and His Kingdom.

Their works are seen through works and mindsets that resist God and His Kingdom.

Compromise.

Ahab and Jezebel are driven by the desire for comfort, power, and control. If they have any convictions, they will lay them down to attract the votes, power, position, or acquisition to get what they want. Just like they did to take the possession of Naboth's vineyard for personal convenience. I have spent a lot of time and stamps writing state officials concerning issues important to God. They always answer out of both sides of their mouth. They say they respect life and decency, but respect the opinions i.e., votes of the proabortion and WOKE crowds more.

They stop at nothing to get their own way.

Do you think we will ever know the truth about the 2020 election or who really leaked the SCOTUS opinion on Roe v. Wade and why? I can tell you the truth. Power hungry politicians will stop at nothing to get their own way. They are driven by demons! They do not care how many riots are started, how many people are killed, how great inflation becomes, or how hard it becomes to find willing workers, an open restaurant, or affordable food and gas.

Increased violence, murder, and lawlessness.

All we have to do is listen to the news and we see how evil is encroaching our communities, even in small cities. Murder, rape, child trafficking, kiddie porn. Evil abounds under Jezebel and Ahab government. We must pray, vote, run for city commission seats, school board, and the like, but there is more.

We must restore biblical submission at every level of society. Ephesians 5:15–6:9 Teaches the work of mutual submission in all human partnerships.

I will only share a few verses of this passage and expound briefly on them.

📖 ¹⁵ See then that you walk circumspectly, not as fools but as wise,

Circumspectly means paying attention to what you are doing, what is going on around you, and how God wants you to influence your part of the world.

📖 ¹⁶ redeeming the time, because the days are evil.

Redeeming refers to buying up each opportunity and using it to advance the Kingdom of God. Think of redeeming the time by comparing the hours you spend in prayer and Bible reading to the hours spent watching television and gaming.

📖 ¹⁷ Therefore do not be unwise, but understand what the will of the Lord *is*.

True wisdom is understanding things from God's point of view, including current political and societal issues.

📖 ¹⁸ And do not be drunk with wine, in which is dissipation.

The word translated "dissipation" above and debauchery or drunkenness in other translations is taken from the compound Greek Word "asotia."

In the Greek, the prefix "a" is used like the English prefix "un." We say born, unborn; fruitful, unfruitful; wise, unwise; etc. "Un" reverses the meaning of the word it is attached to.

The Greek word "sotia" refers to full salvation relating to spiritual, physical, mental, emotional, and financial health. Put the "a" in front of it and you have "asotia" which literally means "full salvation—NOT!"

Paul continued the verse with "but be filled with the Spirit," which brings the fulness of salvation.

📖 ¹⁹speaking to one another in psalms and hymns and spiritual songs, singing and making melody in your heart to the Lord,

The above refers to encouraging one another of like faith.

📖 ²⁰ giving thanks always for all things to God the Father in the name of our Lord Jesus Christ,

Giving thanks in all situations, including disappointing election results and continuing perversion and degradation in society is key to victory. Ungrateful people are seldom victorious.

📖 ²¹ submitting to one another in the fear of God. Ephesians 5:15–21.

This passage begins with a close examination of the outcome of living and governing the way we do. It leads to the promise of being filled with the Holy Spirit and developing an attitude to cooperation which leads to mutual submission. Without taking time to explain it, I will summarize it. If we restore biblical submission two things will happen.

Leaders will submit to the need of their followers.
Followers will submit to the lead of their leaders.

Jezebel and Ahab refuse to submit to the need of their followers. They try to strip godly parents of their right to teach their children what the Bible says about traditional marriage, life begins at conception, the freedom to refuse covid jabs or wearing masks.

Jezebel and Ahab think they have authority to forbid families to gather in their homes for holidays, or visit the dying in nursing homes, or assemble in Churches to worship the Lord. They forget they were elected to represent the people, not control them.

We need to take down the strongholds Jezebel and Ahab.

We need to restore the full authority and responsibility of the traditional family as the bedrock of society. Galatians 5:22–23.

Neither a 5 x7 note nor this 151-page book is adequate to describe what we, as Christ's Ekklesia, is called to do. But when we begin focusing on the things shared here, we can individually and collectively advance the Kingdom of God forcibly in our cities, state, and nation (Matthew 11:12).

Let me end with two safeguards.

Safeguards of Spiritual Warfare:

Put the Spiritual Armor on and keep it on. Ephesians 6:10.

This is crucial. Study and apply the full armor of God. Wear it when you are awake and when you are sleeping. Decree this quote from Derek Prince every morning and night:

"I am redeemed by the blood of the Lamb from the hand of the enemy."

Ask the Lord to rebuke the enemy unless He tells you to.

Jude 9 gives protective instruction when he says,

📖 Yet Michael the archangel, in contending with the devil, when he disputed about the body of Moses, dared not bring against him a reviling accusation, but said, "The Lord rebuke you!" Jude 9.

When doing spiritual warfare, we must not be presumptive. It is dangerous to enter war without the full armor of God and precise instructions from the Lord and from our spiritual authorities.

Michael the archangel was wise when he stayed in the Lord's protective covering and said, "The Lord rebuke you." Rule of Thumb, ask the Lord to rebuke demons and principalities unless He commands you to do so. Either way you remain under God's protection. When we are submitted fully to Jesus, the devil has to go through Him to get to us!

Final Thoughts

It has become increasingly difficult to judge one's character by his or her title. Preachers used to be held in high esteem. Unfortunately, there have been enough high-profile scandals among ministers, clergy have lost their credibility.

Too many base their incessant ranting on social issues according to what they perceive to be true rather than on the Word of Truth. While writing this chapter, I skimmed a news article about a pastor in a neighboring community who made the headlines because someone had destroyed the church's campaign sign promoting the most heinous abortion proposal America has ever seen. No "preacher" who understand the Bible can be pro-abortion!

People claiming to love the Lord and pretending to hold the Bible in high regard, fight for what the Bible says is abomination. They campaign for liberal, leftist, WOKE, and liberal policies and politicians because they are deceived by love tainted ideologies while ignoring the Word of God and the God of the Word.

Some, who claim to follow Jesus fight for so-called rights the Bible clearly states are wrong. My home state's attorney general, in total aberration of her office, states she will not enforce any law restricting abortion, as if she has the power to rewrite law according to her views that the Bible clearly states as reprobate (See Romans 1:24–28 for example.).

In Matthew 5:13, Jesus states the following concerning people of true faith, "You are the salt of the earth; but if the salt loses its flavor, how shall it be seasoned? It is then good for nothing but to be thrown out and trampled underfoot by men."

My hope and prayer is God will speak through this book to draw people back to Himself and to His Word. It will take people from every walk of society to bring the kind of reformation to our communities that God can and will bless.

📖 Repent, then, and turn to God, so that your sins may be wiped out, that times of refreshing may come from the Lord. Acts 3:19 NIV.

📖 So now you need to rethink everything and turn to God so your sins will be forgiven and a new day can dawn, days of refreshing times flowing from the Lord. Acts 3:19 The Voice Bible.

About the Author

Douglas E. Carr was born again in 1972 and entered full-time Christian ministry in 1973. He took his first church in 1976 and worked very hard at the ministry. Every church he pastored grew numerically, even though he lacked the spiritual depth to lead his people from the tree of the knowledge of good and evil into the tree of life.

Doug labored hard, but with limited results, until he broke free from religious bondage and finally began letting Holy Spirit work and through him whenever, wherever, and however he was prompted to by God.

It took a personal loss to bring Doug to where he cried out to better know God personally. After fourteen years of ministry, he was broken and left "professional" ministry for five years. For Doug, it took personal failure to help him realize just how wonderful God's love and grace really are.

Doug was restored to pastoral ministry in 1992 and has been on the quest to know and share the love, acceptance, and forgiveness of God Almighty. He has come to know Holy Spirit personally and has a great desire to lead people into freedom and victory. Now his church is not growing numerically as fast as it used to, but the people are becoming large in the Lord.

God has been good to Doug, blessing him with Pamela, his wonderful wife, helpmate, and partner in ministry since 12-12-93. The very meaning of the numbers (12 represents apostolic and/or governmental fullness) in the date God chose for their wedding was indicative of how they needed to grow together in the ways of Jesus Christ and His Holy Spirit

Doug ministered his first deliverance in the mid-nineties. He soon sensed the call to lead others to freedom and began leading freedom appointments and Free Indeed Seminars.

In 1999, after a forty-day fast, Doug was led to Wagner Leadership Institute where he earned his master's and Doctorate with proficiencies in Deliverance and Intercession. While taking classes there he met Barbara Yoder and soon became part of her Breakthrough Apostolic Ministries Network.

Doug is truly blessed with His wife Pamela, and their five children, twenty-four grandchildren, and a growing number of great-grandchildren. Doug and Pam pastor His House Foursquare Church in Sturgis, Michigan, and continue to minister deep healing and deliverance, as well as lead Freed Indeed Seminars. Their message may be heard on YouTube by date. Put: **His House Church Sturgis** in your web browser and search by date.

Dr. Carr realizes the need to raise up ministers of deep healing and deliverance who will walk in the fullness of the Spirit to bring healing and freedom to those who so desperately need it.

During the Releasing the Glory gathering at Shekinah Regional Training Center, Doug kept hearing *The Great*

Awakening will bring people into the churches who have tattoos and piercings everywhere you can see and many places you should never see. There will be many who have soul ties beyond numbering from recreational sex. Many have been addicted to so many substances they are now addicted to addiction. It is time for Believers to stop being afraid of the devil and his demons and stand up in faith knowing the devil and his demons are afraid of them!"

With this word came two impressions: 1) We need to cast out the corporate spirit of the fear of the devil and demons. 2) God is waiting for the church to be ready to steward the Great Awakening so none will be lost as in the Jesus Movement. This preparation to steward the Awakening includes preparing a few from every church, or at least every city or neighborhood, to be thorough and effective in Deep Inner Healing and Deliverance.

To that end, Doug has launched regional "Equipping and Certification Programs." Currently, a deliverance ministers' intensive program has been developed for Sturgis, Michigan in 2022 and 2023.

Doug and Pam Carr also pastor His House Foursquare Church in Sturgis, Michigan where Pam's greatest call is to release the Presence of God through worship and Doug's greatest call is to equip others to do the work of the ministry in Sturgis, Michiana (Southwest Michigan and Northern India region Pam and I oversee for BAMN), and beyond through books and seminars.

The book you hold in your hands is Doug's thirtieth. Many of his books and other resources are available through Amazon.com, or they can be ordered directly from him.

For more information on Doug's ministry, seminars, or links to his books visit:
www.dcfreedomministry.com

Email: FreedomMinister@yahoo.com

Resources by Dr. Douglas E. Carr

Devotionals:
- *Kingdom Thoughts 101.*
- *Kingdom Thoughts 201.*
- *Light in the Darkness.*

Deliverance:
- *Ask the Doctor about Deliverance.*
- *Beat Me Up Spirits.*
- *Breaking the Octopus Grip of Addiction.*
- *Building on a Sure Foundation After Deliverance.*
- *Busting Through to Greater Freedom.*
- *Divorced! Obtaining Freedom From The Sun & Moon God. Jeanette Strauss & Doug Carr.*
- *Free Indeed ~ Deliverance Ministry.*
- *Free Indeed from Root Spirits.*
- *From Woe is Me to WOW is He!*
- *Holy Spirit as Counselor.*
- *Patterns of Perversity ~ Freedom from Iniquity.*

Discipleship:
- *Choosing Kingdom.*
- *Defining Moments ~ My Journey Toward the Kingdom.*
- *Let's Get Real.*
- *Kingdom Abundance.*

Healing:
- *Kingdom Perspective: Divine Healing.*

Names of God – Prayer:
- *Ancient Keys ~ Special Names.*

Spiritual Gifts: Of God, Gifts, and Men (3 Vols.):
- *Ascension Gifts.*
- *Motivational Charismata Gifts.*

- *Holy Spirit Manifestations.*

Teaching:

- *Breakthrough Essentials.*
- *Getting to the Dirty Rotten Inner Core.*
- *God's Say So versus Man's Know So.*
- *Holidays to Shape Your Life and Transform Your Future.*
- *Making Abundance a Lifestyle*
- *Schematics: God's Blueprint vs Satan's Programming.*
- *Time to Act* – The Enemy Snuck in While We Were Sleeping.

Free Indeed Seminars

Doug also ministers the following seminars individually or part of an Intensive Deliverance Ministers Equipping and Certification program.

- MOD 1 Basic Building Blocks of Deliverance
- MOD 2 Deliverance from Curses, Iniquities, and the Big Five
- MOD 3 Holy Spirit Mending of Broken Hearts
- MOD 4 Free Indeed From Root Spirits
- MOD 5 From Woe is Me to Wow is He!
- MOD 6 Breaking Through to Greater Freedom
- MOD 7 Breaking the Octopus Grip of Addiction.

Doug Carr Freedom Ministries
His House Foursquare Church
410 South Clay Street
Sturgis, MI. 49091

Email FreedomMinister@yahoo.com
Web: www.DCFreedomMinistry.org

www.ingramcontent.com/pod-product-compliance
Lightning Source LLC
Chambersburg PA
CBHW060901280326
41934CB00007B/1136